Writing for the Web

Robert Ashton and Jessica Juby

Robert Ashton is a bestselling business author, social entrepreneur and campaigner. Described as 'human WD40', he helps organizations enjoy becoming more enterprising. He is now a vice patron of the Norfolk Community Foundation after being a trustee for seven years. He is also a patron of Hertfordshire Action on Disability. He started the Robert Ashton Organization Ltd, a social enterprise, to connect newly self-employed people who have valuable skills with organizations needing help.

Jessica Juby has worked for Robert since she left sixth form. Starting as a marketing apprentice, she now handles the everyday running of his office.

Writing for the Web

Robert Ashton and Jessica Juby

First published in Great Britain in 2013 by Hodder & Stoughton. An Hachette UK company.

First published in US in 2013 by The McGraw-Hill Companies, Inc.

This edition published 2013

British Library Cataloguing in Publication Data: a catalogue record for this title is available from the British Library.

Library of Congress Catalog Card Number: on file.

10 9 8 7 6 5 4 3 2 1

The publisher has used its best endeavours to ensure that any Website addresses referred to in this book are correct and active at the time of going to press. However, the publisher and the author have no responsibility for the Websites and can make no guarantee that a site will remain live or that the content will remain relevant, decent or appropriate.

The publisher has made every effort to mark as such all words which it believes to be trademarks. The publisher should also like to make it clear that the presence of a word in the book, whether marked or unmarked, in no way affects its legal status as a trademark.

Every reasonable effort has been made by the publisher to trace the copyright holders of material in this book. Any errors or omissions should be notified in writing to the publisher, who will endeavour to rectify the situation for any reprints and future editions.

Cover image © carlos castilla – Fotolia

Typeset by Cenveo® Publisher Services.

Printed and bound in Great Britain by CPI Group (UK) Ltd., Croydon, CR0 4YY.

Hodder & Stoughton policy is to use papers that are natural, renewable and recyclable products and made from wood grown in sustainable forests. The logging and manufacturing processes are expected to conform to the environmental regulations of the country of origin.

Hodder & Stoughton Ltd

338 Euston Road

London NW1 3BH

www.hodder.co.uk

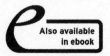

Also available in ebook

Contents

Introduction

Words are important – they are everywhere and form the foundation of our communication with others. Many of us find that writing is easier than saying out loud what we feel. The Internet is becoming faster and, with mobile technology, more readily accessible. There are now more outlets than ever to share your thoughts and feelings the moment they happen. There's no doubt that even more outlets are on the way.

Evidence of this is the rapid sales growth of tablet computers. Not only are they simple to use, but they are ready to use the moment you open the cover. You no longer have to wait for your laptop to fire up. It's: think, press, post!

And that is, of course, both your opportunity and a threat. Yes, you can post pictures and words about events as they happen. At work, this can be a huge bonus. But at midnight on a Friday, when you are having a good time out with friends, it can be all too easy to publish content that in the cold light of the following morning you regret.

Wi-Fi hotspots can now be found all over the country so, even if you haven't got Internet access at home, you can pop down to your local café and take advantage of theirs for free. Few charge these days: they know that the longer they can keep you online, the more coffee you will drink! No matter what your view is of the Internet, it is universally used and increasingly provides an affordable, effective and authentic means of getting your message out to your audience.

We all have the potential to be better writers, but some people will find writing relatively easy – you might even write for pleasure as well as work. Others may need a bit more practice. If you fall into the latter camp, don't worry – take your time, practise and you will get it perfect. Remember that not everyone will, or should, write in the same style. We each have our own style of writing, with favourite words and phrases. Just as with speech, we each have a writing voice.

This book, for example, has two authors. Robert (that's me) is older and a more experienced writer with 15 published books. Jess (that's me) is younger and sees the world very differently from Robert. See if you can spot which sections we wrote individually and which together. As you become familiar with the book, you will begin to see which of us wrote (or said) what.

This book is about much more than just the mechanics of writing, though: you need to make sure you understand your audience. In order to keep your readers interested, responsive and perhaps willing to come back, you have to know what it is they are expecting from you. Then you can keep delivering. Even if your reason for writing is your own personal satisfaction, you will still want readers. As Robert says, writing without a reader in mind is like singing in the bath – likely to annoy more than it pleases!

Using this book

The title of this book challenges you to become comfortable writing for many readers. Words published online may be read by a few, or by many. Just look at how some YouTube films go viral, attracting millions of views. The same thing can happen with words.

This book will give you the confidence to:

▶ improve your writing skills so you can positively influence your online community

▶ understand and follow good online best practice.

In each chapter of this book you will find the following features in addition to the main text:

▶ **Diagnostic test** At the start of every chapter you will find simple flow charts to help you evaluate your skills and thinking in relation to the chapter subject.

▶ **Case study** This will illustrate a success or disaster story for each chapter, showing what went right or wrong, with the goal of helping *you* to get it right and avoid any potential pitfalls.

▶ **Try it now** This is a chance for you to take a break and try out some activities. They will help you practise newly learned skills or carry out necessary research.

▶ **Remember this** These sections will emphasize points you should always bear in mind when writing online.

▶ **Key idea** These focus on important concepts that you need to know.

▶ **Focus points** Sited at the end of each chapter, this list draws your attention to the important points that you will have learned in the chapter.

▶ **Summary and Next step** Also at the end of each chapter, these provide a round-up of what has been covered in the chapter you have just read and what we will go on to cover in the next chapter.

There are plenty of books out there that tell you how to use social media sites and write online. What makes this book unique is that when discussing various aspects of writing for the Web, we will be using the generational gap between us – that's Robert and Jess – to illustrate some of the differences in perception of those aspects. These may be individual opinions or personal memories, but we will show how attitudes to the Web can vary and how they may affect your behaviour online.

This book is ideal for people who either don't have much experience with online writing or who can write but don't know what areas of the Internet they should be focusing on. It doesn't matter what age you are – we will take you through each aspect of writing for the Web from scratch. *Everybody* has the ability to learn.

We have put this book together so that each chapter will take you one step closer to achieving a specific goal. Whether you are writing for websites, social media or other platforms, the end goal is being able to communicate more effectively online, both at work and at home.

Throughout this book, we will refer to the 'project'. This is our generic term for whatever it is you are working on that has prompted you to get online. It may be your business or it may be a personal hobby. Using the term 'project' just keeps it generic.

Business or home?

Finally, we include a few introductory words about the two broad spheres in which you are likely to use your Web writing skills:

▶ **In business** There are few jobs that don't involve using a computer to some extent. For almost all of us, the Internet has become the number-one source of information. It's an amazing place for research. If you are thinking about starting your own business, or are already up and running, you will probably appreciate that the quality and quantity of online coverage your business gets is vital to your success. Your basic business details need to be within easy reach of all those potential customers searching for the products or services you deliver. It will also be used by potential new suppliers and employees. In other words, the more visible your enterprise is online, the more opportunities you will find coming your way.

▶ **At home** The chances are that most of your 'heavy-duty' online writing will be carried out at work, but, with the rise of social media sites, Internet usage at home is sure to increase, too. You may find that your job role doesn't quite satisfy your passions, and in search of an outlet to discuss and develop your interests, you may choose to start an online blog or become a commentator for online magazine sites.

We will be returning to both these areas – business and home – throughout this book.

So, what are you waiting for?

Let's get cracking.

Writing basics

In this chapter you will learn:

- *how the Internet has transformed communication around the globe*
- *the basic writing standards that you will need to keep to if you are to write effectively for the Web – these include well-presented, properly spelled and grammatically correct sentences and paragraphs as well as issues such as avoiding gender bias and offensive language*
- *the importance of clarity and brevity and getting the right tone.*

Self-assessment: What do you want to get out of this book?

Let's run through the first diagnostic test. Start at the top and respond to the statements honestly and read the feedback for the number that your answers lead you to.

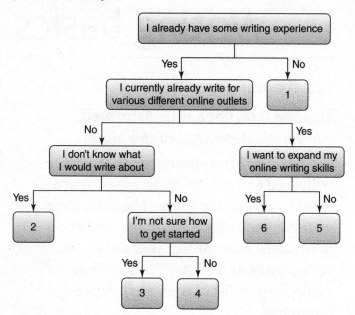

Feedback

1 Don't worry if you have not written much before – practice makes perfect. In this chapter we will run through the basic writing skills that you will need to learn and action when writing for the Web. It's always good practice to draft and edit your text on your PC and then post the final version to the Internet.

2 There are lots of things that you could write about. The key is finding something you are comfortable with, that is relevant to you and likely to be interesting to others. This is especially true when blogging, as you will be planning to write about the same topic for a long time. In each chapter we will cover what it is you should be including.

3 We have covered various online writing outlets in each chapter of this book. From social media to blogging, there are plenty of tips to get you up and running. If there's one area you are particularly interested in, why not start with that chapter once you have finished this one?

4 So you already know what to write about and how to get started. Perhaps your problem is finding the time to get started? Writing online has never been easier – mobile access means you can tweet on the go, and the ability to queue blog posts means you don't even have to be at your computer to publish an article. Maybe you need to brush up on your skills first before actually posting anything online. This chapter will be perfect for you as we cover a lot of dos and don'ts when it comes to writing.

5 There's always room for improvement – nobody is perfect! You will come to learn that the online world is always evolving, so what you know today may not apply in a few months' time. Different sites will become popular as others slowly fade away and you will need to learn how to adapt to write for these new sites.

6 Practise writing using the tips in this chapter and you will be geared up to start writing online. Remember that some people will find it easier than others, simply because we all learn at different speeds. Have patience, invest your time and you will get there.

Journey to a new age

'The world hates change, yet it is the only thing that has brought progress.'

Charles F. Kettering

In the 1960s four universities became joined as they took a step forward that would forever change the way we behave at work and at home. For the first time, they were connected online as a result of a US Department of Defence innovation. However, it wasn't until 1982 that a standardized concept of 'the Internet' (originally 'Internetworking') came into play.

It was in 1989 that British computer scientist and MIT professor Tim Berners-Lee wrote a proposal for what would become the World Wide Web. A year later Berners-Lee joined up with Belgian computer scientist Robert Cailliau at CERN (the European Organization for Nuclear Research) to implement the Hypertext project for the first time. As a result they achieved the first successful communication between a server and a Hypertext Transfer Protocol (HTTP) client via the Internet.

Now, more than 30 years later, there are very few people who don't know what the Internet is or what it does. Those who were, and maybe still are, against it are finding themselves in a society that would struggle to function without it. It has seeped into almost everything we do.

The Internet was once an easy way for a select few to share data with other connected individuals. It's since evolved into something that provides an easy way for everyone to share thoughts, ideas, news and views with the whole world.

On the Web

Robert says...

I was amazed by the first calculator and excited when fax meant I could send documents far faster than the postman. Later, in the early 1990s, I ran a design business. It was at around the time that Macintosh replaced the drawing board. But the only way to deliver digital files to the printer was by motorcycle courier. And then the Internet arrived.

It was initially too slow to allow much more than surfing and email, but as speed increased, so too did its impact on my life. Rather like growing older, the changes were constant and gradual. Speed increased, broadband replaced dial-up and email largely replaced both the post and phone calls. My inbox fills quickly every day; my phone hardly rings.

Today my relationship with the Internet has become deeply personal, intimate even. I am in touch with a huge number of people all the time – from social comment on Facebook to professional debate on LinkedIn. The immediacy of access provided by my iPhone and iPad enables me to tweet a thought the moment it pops into my head, wherever in the world I happen to be.

I now live and work in two parallel worlds – one physical and one online. It's very exciting!

Jess says...

In researching for this book, I imagined that the Internet had been around far longer than it actually has. I was a little bit shocked to discover that it actually only came into play the year before I was born.

My family had a computer before we had the Internet and the distinctive 'dial-up tone' will always be buried in the back of my mind somewhere – that noise is unforgettable. It would signal such an agonizing wait. I would be on tenterhooks, waiting to see if the connection would be made, holding my breath in case it dared refuse (which, living in rural Norfolk, it often did).

Back then, connecting to the Internet would block your phone from receiving calls. Anyone who tried to get through when you were online would hear the engaged tone. This meant that I had to get prior permission from my parents to go online. If they were expecting a call, going on the Internet was a no-no.

Now, all the excitement about loading up Internet Explorer has vanished and my addiction is no longer a Harry Potter fan forum – it's Facebook. The dial-up tone is a long-lost sound, broadband guarantees a connection, and Wi-Fi allows you access wirelessly – but still, it's a story to tell the grandchildren who'll wonder how the devil we coped.

Almost any advert you see or hear, whether it be on TV, radio or in print, will contain a website address. Most now even go so far as to tell you to go online and find the company on

Facebook or follow them on Twitter. Everyday items you buy from the supermarket now have 'QR codes' (Quick Response) printed on the labels which can be scanned with a smartphone to access the Internet to find out more about the product, take part in a competition, or make the most of a special offer.

In August 2011 the UK Office for National Statistics announced that 77 per cent of all households in the UK had access to the Internet in one form or another. This rose to 80 per cent in 2012. So the chances are high that you, your colleagues and your customers already use the Internet. Figure 1.1 shows the increase in number of households with access to the Internet, demonstrating a steady increase over the last 14 years.

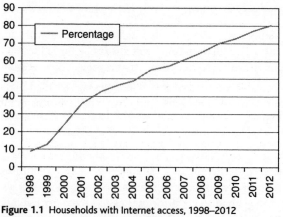

Figure 1.1 Households with Internet access, 1998–2012
(Source: Office for National Statistics)

With the growing popularity of social media sites, and the ease with which you can access information, you cannot ignore them. However, the Internet is about a lot more than watching funny cat videos on YouTube or letting your friends know that you have just got a high score on Angry Birds.

Writing etiquette

It's important to be confident enough to write online – you don't want any bad content coming back in the future to haunt you. Even the most seasoned writer may still find the occasional typo (short for 'typographical error') slipping into their work here and there – even the greats have proofreaders. Don't be afraid of making mistakes – we all make them – but remember that most mistakes can be avoided. Take your time and read everything before you post it on the Internet. In most cases, you can delete comments or edit articles, but there are occasions where you won't have that luxury.

Below are some 'bad habits' or issues you might want to watch out for.

TEXTSPEAK
If you migrated to the Internet from your mobile phone, you may have fallen into the habit of using 'textspeak'. It's quicker to type but can be more difficult for others to understand. You may also use a lot of abbreviations and emoticons. You may even do this at work – in which case, please stop. In the workplace textspeak doesn't look professional, so always type full words and avoid abbreviations. The only place where these are forgivable are on Twitter, where messages, called updates, are limited to 140 characters only (we will cover this in more detail later).

Say u wer 2 get an email written entirely lyk dis tryin 2 sel u a product – would you be impressed? *We* wouldn't be: the email would be regarded as spam and promptly deleted. Being professional means making the effort. Try to get yourself out of this habit and always write in full sentences, whether it's for something personal or for business. If you visited a website that was completely written in textspeak, you would have quite a headache after trying to decipher it. Avoid it completely and you won't find yourself slipping into your old habits.

Try it now: Texting

If you are used to skipping letters in your texts, start using full words from now on – get yourself out of this bad habit and the transition from 'textspeak' to correctly forming words and sentences will be a lot easier. The benefit of this is that you will start using proper words and thus be communicating more clearly.

BAD SPELLING AND GRAMMAR

Not every single person finds it easy to express themselves in writing. There are plenty of reasons why this might be. You may be dyslexic; dyslexia is a broad term applied to learning disabilities that affect fluency in reading or writing, with some cases more serious than others. You might have disliked English at school, or just always found writing a chore, never being able to get the hang of it.

The majority of publishing programs (such as Microsoft Word) come with built-in checks that will alert you when a word is spelled incorrectly or when a sentence appears to be grammatically incorrect. If you struggle with spelling and grammar, write everything in a publishing program first until you get it right, before copying and pasting it online. You can even get a friend or a family member to read through what you have written first, before it becomes part of the public domain.

Alternatively, you can purchase voice recognition software. This will transcribe what you say into text. It's still worth getting someone to read through what it produces in case it has 'misheard' you. Checking it will also make sure the text flows well.

RAMBLING

It can be useful to drop in the odd anecdote or two but, when reading back what you have written, ask yourself the question: 'So what?' When reading over your article, if you find something that isn't interesting or relevant to the rest of the article, simply delete it. Fewer words can actually mean more!

Did you have one of those teachers at school who would start off mentioning something that was actually relevant to the curriculum but it would somehow turn into a personal life story? It was rarely fascinating and almost never relevant to those trying to learn. Don't be like them!

Remember this: The goal of writing

The sole purpose of your writing is to communicate clearly, inform, influence and perhaps entertain.

PUNCTUATION

Another one of our pet hates, when it comes to emailing in particular, are those messages that contain no punctuation – for example:

> hi there im emailing you about your book that I just read its very good and I am thinking about buying another one from your store could you possibly send me a link to the right place so I can buy it thanks talk soon bye

Again, publishing programs alert you when they can detect a sentence that hasn't been punctuated correctly. Look out not just for missing commas, full stops and capital letters, but apostrophes – missing here in 'im' and 'its'. The apostrophe signals that the words 'I am' and 'it is' have been shortened and that there are letters missing. Read your text back to yourself as it is – out loud may help more. If you find yourself putting in full stops and commas when you speak, then make sure they are actually there in the text.

Key idea: The golden rule of punctuation
Too much is almost always better than not enough.

EXPERIENCE AND KNOWLEDGE

Some people will see their lack of knowledge and experience as an issue, but the solution is simple. It doesn't matter if you have never written anything before or if you have written lots. You don't need a qualification to be able to market yourself online. This is because most sites you will use in your online journey have useful 'help' areas, FAQs and user forums. You will find that you can usually teach yourself how to use them.

Remember this: In the public domain
Anything and everything you publish online is in the public domain. It is accessible by everyone. Don't post anything that may be damaging to you or others. Remember that people have found themselves in prison for posting inappropriate content online.

Writing standards

Your writing should read like something you would say aloud. The only difference is that you have got the ability to edit text and omit the 'ums' and 'ers'. Some people feel the need to make their writing more formal than their speech. But the danger in this is that you will no longer sound like yourself and, worse, appear insincere or not committed to the message you are communicating. Just as you should always 'say it like it is', so, too, should you 'write it like it is'!

Here's a further list of writing good-practice points. Make a note of them and try to follow them as much as you can. It will make your writing far more effective and far less likely to provoke criticism:

▶ **Avoid gender bias.** Use 'they' and 'their' instead of assuming a gender. Although these pronouns are plural, it's now common to use them with singular nouns to avoid gender bias.

▶ **Keep it clean.** Never use swear words in any professional content.

▶ **Stay away from clichés.** A cliché is a phrase that tends to be overused, such as 'blushing bride' or 'run it up the flagpole'. Try to avoid them.

▶ **Avoid hype.** This tends to sneak into sales pitches. Your readers will detect this immediately, so don't exaggerate or overstate your sales presentation. It's better to put yourself in the shoes of the typical buyer and use the language they would use to describe the product, service or event you are writing about.

▶ **Stay focused.** Be brutal and simply cut out paragraphs and sentences that wander away from your overall message. Editing is the key to good writing. Fewer words will often convey more meaning. If in doubt about a phrase, sentence or even paragraph, cut it!

▶ **Be positive.** Fewer words are used in positive statements than in negative ones and it will keep the overall tone of your writing lighter. Everybody prefers success to failure, so make your writing positive and about success.

▶ **Stick to one tense** (past, present or future) – don't switch between them unless it's required by the context.

Remember this: Point of view

First person ('I' or 'we') This is where you are writing about yourself, your experiences and your views. The first-person writer has credibility; they are telling you what they think.

Second person ('you') This is where you are telling your reader what you think they need to know or do. It is best used for instructions.

Third person ('he' or 'she') This is used to describe what others are seeing, thinking and doing. It is the form used most frequently when writing fiction. Not surprisingly, if you write in the third person, people may question your personal commitment to what you are describing.

People who are not confident writers have an unfortunate habit of using big words and clunky phrases. We have all had letters signed off with the meaningless phrase 'Assuring you of our best intentions at all times.' It's a phrase that seems to be seen then copied by people who feel the need somehow to pretend to be someone they are not.

Online, there are no secrets, so pretending to be anything other than yourself is difficult to maintain and pointless to consider. What's vital is that your uniqueness comes over in everything you write online. Your writing needs to reflect your style, personality and background. Even if you are writing on behalf of an organization, you have to be yourself. Organizations do not have brains, fingers or voices. They are teams of *people*, and people connect with and do business with other people.

Imagine that you work in the support department of a government agency fielding enquiries from members of the public. There will be the factual information you have to accurately convey. There will also be opportunities to appear human, concerned and, perhaps where appropriate, compassionate. People always respond better to people, so always, always make sure your own humanity is visible through your writing.

Another key point to remember is that the Internet is global. While English is almost universally spoken, for many it is a second or third language. There is no point in using words that might not be understood or, worse, create ambiguity. Avoid the temptation to be 'clever' and use big words, unless, that is, you go on to explain their meaning. For example, an economist might write about an oligopoly (a market dominated by a small number of suppliers). Oligopoly is the right word for them to use, as the explanation shows. You can educate as well as inform.

When you express your views, ideas and concerns online, there is one final important point to make. Just suppose you overslept, woke to find that your dog had chewed a hole in your favourite coat, and then you spilled your breakfast coffee down your front and finally arrived at work in a foul mood. That kind of thing happens to us all. But however angry, grumpy or hard done by you feel, it should not be reflected in anything you write online. For one thing, your rant will remain on view for all to see. And then there's the simple fact that people want the stuff they read to cheer them up, not make them feel worse. So, however down you feel, always, always write positively about everything.

I can't stress this point enough. For almost everyone, the downside usually comes to mind first. That's not to say we are all naturally depressives. It's more that we all find the negative harder to deal with and so naturally focus on that side of things before moving on to the bright side of life. Read and tweak everything you write before you post it, to make it just that little bit more upbeat.

🔑 Key idea: Tone

If you are trying to be serious, then don't attempt to crack a joke. If you want your writing to be light-hearted, then avoid sombre words. Decide what tone you want for your article and stick to it. Remember that you can be funny without being flippant and serious without making your reader burst into tears.

ELIMINATING THE EXCESS

When you were a student you will have been asked to write essays of, say, 5,000 words. If you were a little uncertain of your subject, you would waffle a bit to make what you were writing stretch to fit the word count you had been set.

Nobody now will read wasted or excess words. Here are our top five tips for avoiding them:

1 Use **titles and subtitles** to break up text. You can then omit any introductory sentences in the new sections.

2 Use **bullet points** to help keep your points short and to avoid the repetition of an introductory sentence. For example, instead of bullet-pointing the above standards, we would have had to have a new sentence for each one that began 'Another standard is...'

3 Avoid **needless phrases** such as 'in order to', 'all of a sudden' or 'as a matter of fact'. Just use 'to', 'suddenly' or 'truly' instead, to avoid the waffle.

4 Remove any **redundant words** that repeat what you have already said. Common phrases such as 'close proximity' and 'past experience' can be reduced to just one word.

5 Remove any **unconfident** (such as 'seems', 'possibly', 'sort of', 'may') or **arrogant** ('indeed', 'of course', 'surely', 'exactly', 'obviously') -sounding words. They are unnecessary and your content will read much better without them.

SIMPLE SENTENCES AND PARAGRAPHS

Keep your sentences short and to the point – we have just covered how to get rid of unnecessary words, so don't let any sneak into your text. Long sentences are harder to read.

Every time you draft the word 'and', consider replacing it with a full stop. For example:

> On Sunday afternoon we took the children to the zoo and saw the animals, many of which were being fed because by coincidence we arrived at exactly the right time. (*30 words*)

> On Sunday afternoon we took the children to the zoo. We saw the animals. Luckily, we arrived at feeding time. We took some great photographs. (*25 words*)

Paragraphs don't need to be long. They can contain as few as two sentences. A paragraph needs to make a single point. If that point needs detailed explanation, a second paragraph can provide it.

Paragraphs show people when it is a good time to pause. The reader will scan a paragraph quickly, then pause to absorb its meaning before moving on. If your paragraphs are long and unwieldy, they will be harder to read and understand.

Like sentences, the phrases and words you use should be easy to understand and quick to process. When proofreading your text, if you find yourself having to reread sentences to understand their meaning, you need to edit them.

If you are stumbling on something you have written, imagine the difficulty your readers will have. Your readers shouldn't need to use a dictionary to process what you have written. Use everyday words and avoid reaching too often for the thesaurus. If you do use unusual or technical words, be sure to explain their meaning.

If you use an acronym (e.g. AA, AONB, etc.), think about whether your audience will know what the letters stand for. Never assume that your readers will know what an acronym stands for. It is good practice to spell out the acronym in full the first time you use it. For example:

> It is an Area of Outstanding Natural Beauty (AONB).

Don't do this every time the acronym turns up, though, as your sentences will appear clunky and will be longer than they need to be.

Key idea: Metaphor

Good writing paints pictures in the reader's mind. When explaining something quite complicated, comparing it with something the reader probably knows well will make it easier to understand. For example, you might describe the difference between marketing and sales like this: 'Marketing is sending your girlfriend chocolates and flowers, and sales is asking her to marry you.'

Remember this: Action!

Most copy you read – whether it be online or in print – will attempt to persuade you to do something. It might be to buy a product or simply click a link to discover more – all writing has a *purpose*. Below are four of the most common online instructions you will come across; sometimes they are quite obvious, while at others they are much more subtle:

* Read me
* Click me
* Buy me
* Sign up.

Try it now: What makes you act?

Think about the last time you were online. What did you do? What sites did you visit and what action did you take on those sites? What was it that made you take that action? Was it a clear, direct message on the website that told you to do something? Was there an obvious incentive that prompted you to take action? You should bear these reasons in mind when it comes to writing your own online content. You will need to decide on the action you want your readers to take. Finally, the text you write needs to encourage them to do just that.

Finding your voice

Across all the online platforms covered in this book, you need to speak in the same voice. Here are some top tips you can apply in all your online writing:

▶ **Make it clear.** You really do need to 'say it like it is'. Avoid euphemisms or beating about the bush. Just write what's on your mind, or what you want to implant in your reader's mind.

▶ **Keep it short.** Words take time to read and people are quick to lose interest. The fewer words you use, the more likely people are to read and understand them all.

▶ **Make it simple.** An expert is someone who can explain the complex in simple language that all can understand. It's arrogant to use 'industry speak' and it might exclude people you actually need to influence.

Try it now: Write a sample piece for the Web

✻ Think of something really simple you can easily write about. Perhaps it's a recent memory or an important life goal.
✻ Now write 200 words as if you were going to publish it online.
✻ Next, read it through and edit it, referring back to this chapter. Try to incorporate all the tips we have mentioned. Do you keep to one consistent style? Are your sentences short and easy to process? Have you started a new paragraph each time you change point?
✻ Finally, be brave and get someone close to you to read it and give you their honest feedback.

In it for the long haul

Depending on your current skills and experience, the amount of effort you need to put into improving your online presence will vary. Obviously, if you have no experience whatsoever, then it will take considerably longer than someone who has had several online marketing roles, simply because you are starting from scratch. That's why, as with any other task, you must be committed to the end goal – otherwise it will seem like a pointless exercise if you can't see the benefits. But don't feel downhearted by this: no matter how strong or weak your skills are, there will always be someone else in the same boat as you, if not further behind!

Some key statistics

GET ONLINE

The following figures were released in the August 2012 report 'Internet Access – Households and Individuals', issued by the UK's Office for National Statistics:

- ► 80 per cent of households had access to the Internet (up 3 per cent on the previous year), which represents 21 million people.

- ► 93 per cent of those with Internet access have broadband, whereas just 1 per cent are still using dial-up.

- ► Just 2 per cent of adult respondents had used a computer between two months to a year ago compared to the majority (82 per cent), who had used a computer in the last three months.

- ► 67 per cent of those who had used a computer in the past three months had used it daily.

- ► By age group, the majority of those who had used a computer in the past three months were between 16 and 24 years old and 25 and 44 years old (both 96 per cent).

- ► The majority of those who had not used a computer at all were in the 65-and-over age group (44 per cent), but this is down on the figures for 2006, when 65 per cent of the 65-and-over age group had never used a computer.

SOCIAL MEDIA GIANTS

- ► Facebook was founded in 2004. On 14 September 2012 it reported that it had hit a total of 1 billion active monthly users (including 600 million monthly mobile users).

- ► Twitter began in 2006 and five years later, in 2011, broke the 100 million worldwide users barrier. Twitter announced it had some 10 million UK users in May 2012.

- LinkedIn reached 100 million users worldwide in March 2011, eight years after its launch. LinkedIn announced that it had more than 9 million UK users in April 2012.

- Facebook reached 30 million UK users in March 2011 – the UK Facebook users now represent around 49 per cent of the total UK population.

Case study: Charlotte Gunnell, Cavatica Copy (www.cavatica.co.uk)

Although Charlotte has a degree in journalism, it was her work with a website design agency that sparked her true interest in writing online content. She set up Cavatica Copy as an outlet to help her develop search engine optimization (SEO) skills and practise writing.

Charlotte regularly reads online content from other writers to help her learn what it is about their writing that either draws her in or pushes her away: 'Everyone has their strengths. It's the best way to learn what works and what doesn't.' Before you take your first idea and start writing, Charlotte recommends looking at what other people have said on that subject to see what they've missed. Bridge the gap and you will then have written something that your audience has never seen before.

She also counsels brevity: 'The one thing I would avoid doing completely would be to use more words than necessary in order to try and make your point, or to fill a space. Not only do long paragraphs look daunting, but waffle is also very difficult to read and distracts from your point. Use one word if one word will do. Be brutal with your editing; cut words, sentences and even whole paragraphs if they are not necessary. Also cut anything that repeats what you have said before in a different way.'

Charlotte really does practise what she preaches. She's found that, by promoting her writing skills online in an easily accessible blog, she stands out when looking for jobs and other opportunities.

Proving that publishing some great online copy can really pay off, she says, 'I even helped someone else get a job by asking him to write a guest blog post for me; he put the post on his CV and got his dream job a few weeks later.'

Focus points

The main points to remember from this chapter are:

* Everything you put online can be read by every other person on the planet, one way or another.
* When writing, you need to provide clarity, motivation and purpose to keep your audience reading.
* Proofread everything you write, even if you have used the spellchecker.
* You must be dedicated to the end goal, otherwise you won't push through to succeed.
* Practice makes perfect!

Summary

We have masses of knowledge at our fingertips within a matter of mere seconds. So what if you have got your own knowledge to share? This book will help you work out how best to present it, where to reach out with it, who to share it with and how.

You have picked up this book and have therefore realized that improving your online communication can help you spread your own message – whether it be a business or a personal message. The Internet can make you or break you, so it's always best to know both *what* you are doing and the *consequences*. Any mistakes could be costly, and we will give you some examples of how the Internet can quickly turn an audience against you. We will also flag up some danger zones that you will need to be on the lookout for as you progress through the different areas covered in this book.

When you have made your way through the book, but not necessarily in the order we have written it, the quality of your online presence and the effectiveness of your communication will have significantly increased. Our chapters are plainly titled so you can simply dip in and out of the book to cover the areas you are most interested in, as and when you feel like it. We recommend, however, that you read the whole book to ensure that you and/or your project are covering all its online bases. We don't want you missing out on anything – we include important advice that you won't want to skip.

→ **Next step**
In the next chapter we will take things right back to basics and look at your current skills and abilities, what you are already doing online, and what you should be doing.

Your message

In this chapter you will learn:

- ▶ *how to look for what is already online about you or your company – there's probably more than you think!*
- ▶ *the principal motivations for establishing an online presence*
- ▶ *how to identify and reach your target audience*
- ▶ *how a successful competitor can help you create an effective online presence*
- ▶ *how to create a basic plan detailing your online strategy.*

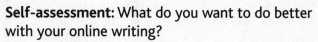

Self-assessment: What do you want to do better with your online writing?

Before you tackle this chapter, we need to check your understanding of what you have just learned from the introduction. Start with the first box of this flow chart, and answer 'yes' or 'no' as you progress and follow the arrows. If you find yourself answering 'no' at any point, go back to the relevant section in the introduction – it will ensure you are on the right path! By the end of this chapter, you will be able confidently to answer 'yes' to every question.

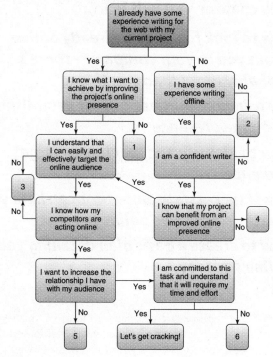

I already have some experience writing for the web with my current project

Yes → I know what I want to achieve by improving the project's online presence

No → I have some experience writing offline

No → **2**

Yes → I am a confident writer

No

Yes → I understand that I can easily and effectively target the online audience

No → **1**

No → **3**

Yes → I know how my competitors are acting online

Yes → I know that my project can benefit from an improved online presence

No → **4**

Yes → I want to increase the relationship I have with my audience

Yes → I am committed to this task and understand that it will require my time and effort

No → **5**

Yes → Let's get cracking!

No → **6**

Feedback

1 You have probably picked up this book because you have lost motivation and need to get back on track. You will learn that it's important for you to stay focused on your overall goal because only then will you see the worth of investing your time and effort in improving your online communication.

2 Having not had much experience at writing or just having not practised it, you may not feel confident enough to publish anything publicly online. Take a look again at our tips in the introduction and remember that practice makes perfect.

3 When it comes to working out who your target audience is, research is vital. Pay particular attention to the 'Understanding your audience' section in this chapter. We will walk you through a task that will take you closer to knowing who you will be writing for.

4 If you are not sure of the benefits of improving your online communication, we have covered them in Chapter 1; take another look if you can't remember them.

5 A good interaction with your audience will improve your chances of support, either in kind or financially through sales of services and products. Sales can be either one-off purchases or repeated; if you rely on repeat sales, your customer retention needs to be high and good interaction with your customers will increase the chances of this happening.

6 Even if you delegate the task (and not dump it on someone!), you will need to check on whoever is handling it to ensure that it runs smoothly.

Why people build their online presence

'The Internet is becoming the town square for the global village of tomorrow.'

Bill Gates

You picked this book up for a reason – to improve the quality of your written communication online and therefore improve your online presence. But what's your overall aim? What do you want to get out of more effective online activity? In general, you will have one of three reasons:

1 to generate enquiries

2 to strengthen relationships

3 to build a brand or profile.

However, for some, the answer may run a little deeper. One thing is certain – the better you know what's driving you to communicate more effectively online, the more dedicated you will be to achieving it.

The deeper question you must ask yourself is this: What will for me be the most important result if I become more articulate online? It might be that your career will develop, or that an organization you own or manage does better. Alternatively, you might simply want to present yourself more confidently to potential life partners.

1 GENERATING ENQUIRIES

The Internet is the first port of call for almost anybody researching almost anything. You can bet that if someone hears about your project and wants to know more, the first place they head to will be their Web browser. Remember that of those who access the Internet, 77 per cent are trying to find information about goods or services.

To make it easy for people to find you online, you need to cover as many bases as possible. You, your work and perhaps your organization need to be mentioned in as many places as possible. For example, you should be listed in directories, described in blogs and profiled on social media sites.

If someone goes online to find out more about you and finds nothing, you may have lost an opportunity. The same is true if people are looking for what you do. Imagine that an editorial researcher is looking for an expert comment on a specialist subject, let's say taxidermy. They will search for taxidermists and then dig deeper to find one who is articulate and interesting. If that's you, then a TV appearance might be imminent. If you are not, you will be surprised to see another taxidermist on TV and wonder how they pulled off such a PR coup!

Remember, too, that often, when someone searches online, they don't know specifically what they are looking for. They will search using generic words and phrases. The better you understand the words people search with, and use them yourself online, the more visible you will become.

Good SEO (search engine optimization) can help. But it is not a cure for poorly written content. Both are important, but what you write is most important of all.

Why is this important?

Every person offering a saleable service or product knows how vital enquiries are. They are the opportunity to turn a lead into a sale. No enquiries mean no sales, and no sales mean no income. If you are selling anything, the messages your online content conveys need to be:

- **S** pecific – I know exactly what you are offering and to whom

- **M** eaningful – I know what it will do for someone like me

- **A** ccessible – I don't need to be an expert to understand what this is about

- **R** elevant – I can quickly see how this is going to help me

- **T** ime-limited – there is a sense of urgency – I need to decide and then act soon!

SMART!

2 STRENGTHENING RELATIONSHIPS
Building and maintaining good customer relationships has never been so easy. But that doesn't mean you can take sites such as Facebook and Twitter for granted. It's terribly easy to let people know what you are thinking. Getting feedback, however, has to be your goal.

Importantly, social media sites enable your supporters, customers, friends and colleagues to:

- show their support, perhaps by 'liking' your pages or adding comments

- add endorsements and reviews – of you, your projects, products and services

- Refer and introduce you to people within their network but outside yours.

Equally, you can show support to others in the same way. In fact, writing flattering reviews of people, places and products can win you reciprocal affirmation. However, you must always be honest and objective.

Twitter provides the best examples. Tweet a negative comment about a large company and within minutes someone from their online team will have contacted you, wanting to know what went wrong. Is that over the top, or just good customer service? Whatever your view, it shows that an organization is on the ball. Check out the Twitter chapter for more on this.

Of course, it's not just social media. Using the Web, you can send out client satisfaction surveys to your database of customers – but don't make these too in-depth. People will be far more likely to tick a few boxes and give short answers to a few questions than spend 15 minutes filling out a questionnaire.

Why is this important?

For us all, reputation is everything. Reputations can be won or lost within hours online. That's why it's so important to be constructive and positive about others. And it's even more important to encourage others to write things that are positive and constructive about you.

For example, imagine you are the manager of a day centre for older people. You might:

▶ link with and support other service providers to older folk

▶ ask your service users and especially their younger carers to post positive reviews about your service

▶ encourage online discussion about relevant 'hot topics', so that you are seen to be progressive and receptive to new ideas.

Part of any customer's experience is the interaction they have with the supplier. A good example of this is Amazon, where every purchase is followed by an invitation to review both the product and the process. Amazon and eBay also use customer feedback to give vendors star ratings. The more stars you have, the more trustworthy you are considered to be.

Reputation is most important when you are handling other people's money. It doesn't matter if you are running an online shop, fundraising for a charity or working as an investment fund manager, people will always be at their most cautious when asked to trust you with their cash.

3 BUILDING A BRAND OR PROFILE

Your reputation can, to a large extent, be presented as your brand. Brands are in many ways 'short cuts' that convey a lot in very few words or images. Think about Apple's reputation for ground-breaking innovation, or Virgin's for challenging monopolistic markets, reducing prices and widening consumer choice.

In order to even start thinking about this, you must know what identity you want, for yourself personally or your organization. It will confuse your customers if you are changing your brand or profile every six months. You need to create a consistent profile and then build on it. Then, once the idea is firmly in your head, you can start styling the way you write, how you write, where you write and so on, so that this ties in with the image you want to portray.

Why is this important?

A recognizable brand or profile is important if you want to be known or your business to be known – for your credibility.

Key idea: Brand vs. profile

Your brand is a summary of your values. Your profile is how you present yourself, in words and images. The more closely these align, the better people will understand what you do and what you stand for.

Self-assessment: Why do you want to move into online world?

Take a look at the flow chart below. Follow the statements on the right and answer honestly. The chart will help you figure out your best reason for making a move into the online world and it gives some basic tips and advice.

Make a note, mental or otherwise, about why you are getting online – you may find that more than one reason applies or that, as you progress through the book, the reason changes. You will also need this/these reason(s) for a task later on in this chapter.

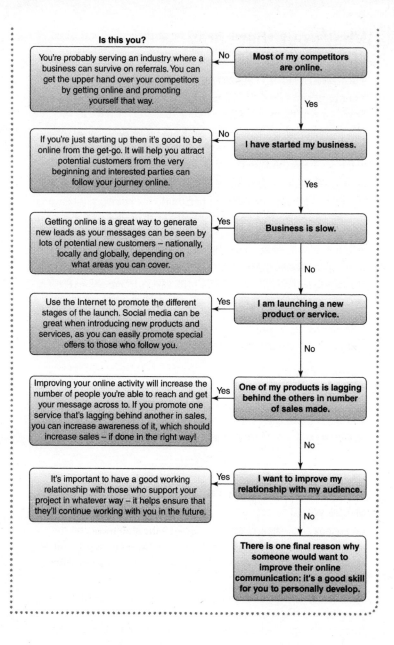

Is this you?

Most of my competitors are online.

No → You're probably serving an industry where a business can survive on referrals. You can get the upper hand over your competitors by getting online and promoting yourself that way.

Yes ↓

I have started my business.

No → If you're just starting up then it's good to be online from the get-go. It will help you attract potential customers from the very beginning and interested parties can follow your journey online.

Yes ↓

Business is slow.

Yes → Getting online is a great way to generate new leads as your messages can be seen by lots of potential new customers – nationally, locally and globally, depending on what areas you can cover.

No ↓

I am launching a new product or service.

Yes → Use the Internet to promote the different stages of the launch. Social media can be great when introducing new products and services, as you can easily promote special offers to those who follow you.

No ↓

One of my products is lagging behind the others in number of sales made.

Yes → Improving your online activity will increase the number of people you're able to reach and get your message across to. If you promote one service that's lagging behind another in sales, you can increase awareness of it, which should increase sales – if done in the right way!

No ↓

I want to improve my relationship with my audience.

Yes → It's important to have a good working relationship with those who support your project in whatever way – it helps ensure that they'll continue working with you in the future.

No ↓

There is one final reason why someone would want to improve their online communication: it's a good skill for you to personally develop.

What's out there now

Even if you or your projects have no website or social media accounts, there will be information about you already out there on the World Wide Web. Search engines are now so sophisticated that even obscure, tangential references to you can easily be found.

That's why it's so important for you to manage the way your profile builds across the Internet. People searching for you will be presented with a list of references, each linking back to the source. Scanning the search results will create an overall impression. You can influence that impression by making sure that material you post around the Internet complements, rather than contradicts, other content.

Now think about whether you have got any of the following. You will need your log-in details for some of them at later stages in the book:

▶ website

▶ blog

▶ directory listings

▶ Twitter account

▶ LinkedIn account

▶ Facebook account and/or Page/Group for the project.

Understanding your audience

Not only do you want to influence a specific audience, perhaps industry figures, friends and customers, but they must be interested in you, too. You won't know who they all are, but you will know what they are – or, at least, what interests they are likely to have.

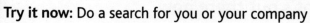

Try it now: Do a search for you or your company

Open up your Internet browser and head to your usual search engine. Type your company name or your own name in double quote marks. For example, if your business name is ABC Gardening, you would type "ABC Gardening" into the search box. If we were searching for new comment on Robert, we'd type "Robert Ashton" into the search box.

This forces the search engine to see your search phrase as a single entry rather than defaulting to seeing each individual word as a phrase you want to look up. This would stop any results coming up that only include the terms 'ABC' or 'Gardening'; instead, the results would list only articles that contain the term 'ABC' followed directly by 'Gardening'. You may have already used this technique when you were researching possible business names to avoid sharing a name with someone else.

This task will be easier if you have got a very specific business name – more common ones will bring up listings for those businesses that share your name. If you are finding more than one business crop up with your business name, narrow the search further by adding a location outside the quoted phrase – for example "ABC Gardening" & Bedford.

The ampersand (&) asks the search engine to list only references that contain both phrases or words. You can keep adding '&' symbols to further refine your search – for example "ABC Gardening" & Bedford & "bedding plants". This will then show a result only if ABC Gardening has been promoting bedding plants online.

Have a scroll through the results. You may find that you attempted to set up a Twitter account, gave up and forgot about it. You will be surprised by what a search on your own name can reveal. Mostly, you will probably find yourself in directory listings.

It's still good to check because there may be the odd mention someone has given you that you weren't aware of. Don't spend too much time having a look through the results, though – if you don't find anything in the first two pages of results, move on!

If you use Google, you can set up 'Google Alerts'. These will send you an email listing all new references to your search term as often as you choose. So you might use this to monitor your own profile, your organizations or a favourite brand. You set up Google Alerts by following the links from the Google home page.

Key idea: Getting noticed

The whole reason for putting information online is in the hope that someone will read it and then act on it.

Try it now: Think about your audience

Take a moment to think about your audience. What kinds of people would be most interested in your project? Are they single or married? Male or female? Old or young? Are they parents, motorists, musicians, unemployed? If you fit the profile of your audience, think about what magazines you read or websites you visit – might your customers read and visit the same? Make a copy of the chart below and fill in as much detail as you can. In the top box, write about how you imagine their personality to be. Use the questions above as a starter to get you going. Then do some research into what magazines, blogs or websites they might visit. Open your browser and type relevant keywords, such as a personality trait followed by magazine/blog/website. For example, if your audience is passionate about different types of cheese, you could search for 'cheese lovers blog'.

My audience are:

Websites	Magazines	Blogs

Even if you are writing online socially, you will want to be read mostly by people with whom you share interests and experiences. They are the most likely to lend their support to your projects, either by buying something or by sharing their own views with you. Online, just as in the real world, we get along best with people with whom we have things in common.

Remember this: Reach your audience

You need to make sure that your information is put in places where those people can easily find it and see how it is relevant to them.

For example, you wouldn't necessarily write an article about different types of cheese and send it to a motoring blog site. The two subject matters have nothing in common; the people who visit the motoring site are looking for new car reviews and aren't interested in which cheese smells the best. You would need to send the article to places that would frequently attract cheese lovers. There would be an exception if you discovered that the blog site was running a feature on picnics to pack in the car – the readers may then be interested to know which smelly cheeses to avoid packing in an enclosed space.

If you struggled with the previous activity, move on to the next section to read about your competition – profiling them is the best way to learn what it is you should be doing.

Losing to the competition

It's a bad idea to be offline when your competition is online. The online world is constantly changing and you don't want to be left behind. You don't want to be the only business in your sector or blogger that's updating Myspace but is nowhere to be found on Facebook. Don't think you have to be the leader of the pack, though – you would have to have exclusive inside information to be ahead of the game. Do listen to what people are saying about online activity – the statistics speak for themselves.

You need to create an online presence that gives people a good first impression of you and your project. Many customers will see this online presence first, and they may not ever meet you face to face or even speak to you. Bad press, slang on your website, and dishing out abuse to critics on social media sites are going to put people off using your products or services – or offering you a job.

Try it now: Research a competitor

Remember the reason why you need to get your business online? Take that reason and look at how a well-established competitor has done the same thing. For example, if you are launching a new product/service, take a look online at how your competitors have launched new products/services.

If you are just in the process of starting up, find a competitor in the same position. If you are looking to become a respected commentator on a certain subject, take a look at who's commenting a lot now on that subject. If you know the names of your competitors, use the search engine tips in the 'Try it now' earlier in this chapter to find more specific results.

Start a mind-map™ with your reason for getting online in the centre and draw off all the activities your competitor did when doing the same thing. Were they featured in an online blog post? Did they launch a social media campaign? Were they running any special offers or competitions? If you have got more than one reason for improving your online communication, then do more than one mind-map™. Whatever positive moves your competitor has made, you should definitely be looking at doing them, too.

One thing that you may have noticed about your competition is the style in which they write, especially if they've got a large brand they are promoting. Their website, blogs and social media posts should all read in a similar way – the style will be the same all the way across the board. This helps reinforce one very important message they are trying to put across: 'We are professional'. Your tone, phrasing and message need to be consistent.

What to avoid

Here are some other things you should consider before asserting your online presence:

▶ **Conflicting messages** If there's an idea that you want to promote, make sure you understand the idea yourself. You don't want to be giving one impression on Monday and then a different one by the end of the week!

▶ **Firing back** You are likely to get some form of criticism, no matter what you post online. It's a fact of life that you can't please everyone – don't make a situation worse by getting into an argument with someone online. Thank them for their feedback and move on – or, if you can, just ignore them.

▶ **Getting addicted** It can be a really big distraction having social media sites such as Twitter and Facebook open as you work. The day can waste away while you sit in front of your screen feeling the need to check every update as it comes in. You really don't need to – you can get alerts set up for the most important updates. The world won't end if you miss something.

▶ **Jargon overkill** If the project you are working on contains many technical terms or uncommon phrases that not everyone has heard of, it's best to avoid these where possible or at least offer an explanation of what the word or phrase means. If someone can't understand what you are writing about, they won't continue reading!

Your priorities

As we mentioned earlier, some online places will be more useful to certain people than others. These are:

▶ a website

▶ accounts with the main social media websites (Twitter, Facebook and LinkedIn)

▶ local online/media directory listings if you are seeking business.

You may also wish to start a blog, either as a separate blogging platform to your website or as a built-in one. Whether you should blog or not depends on your interests, audience and projects. You may wish to write a blog that details the progress of a project, or use it to provide your commentary on current affairs in your sector. That way, providing what you write is relevant and timely, you can be positioned as an authority. If you haven't got any news or views to share then you most likely won't need a blog and can keep updates posted to your website. The golden rule is: If you truly have nothing to say, remain silent!

Measuring success

There are a number of measures of success when you evaluate the impact of your increased online activity. One that is often overlooked is the boost to your own self-esteem. There's something really satisfying about knowing that others are reading and reacting to what you have written.

More specific measures of success will relate to the goals you set in the first place. Are you looking for more sales, career growth, industry recognition or simply to widen your network? Each of these can be measured by the numbers of people who choose to connect, comment or link with you. Remember that you also want people to identify themselves where possible – more on this in later chapters.

In business, if you are selling a product or service, the most obvious way of measuring success is noticing an increase in sales. If you are publishing articles on a blog or website, you will notice an increase in page views, site visits, comments and feedback.

For any kind of project, success will be measured by how many enquiries you get. The more successful you are, the more people will be showing an interest in what you have to offer. You may even find that your project becomes a real hit as a result of your online activity. For example, other blogs, magazines and websites may want to feature it and provide coverage, either written by them or supplied by you.

Remember this: Measure your success

Success can be measured by an increase in the following:
* website visits
* blog post views
* general enquiries via telephone, email, post or online contact form
* sales
* additional coverage as people share your views
* invitations to take part in projects and events
* backlinks (other sites that link back to you – we cover these further in the next chapter).

Finally, never underestimate serendipity. Sometimes the most amazing opportunities can come your way as a direct result of something you have said online. You never know who is going to read what you have posted. The best offers always come from those you would never, ever normally think to, or have the opportunity to, contact.

A plan of action

Now that we have taken a look at what's already online about you, who your target audience is, and what your rivals may be doing, it's time to start doing something yourself.

Try it now: Make plans

The table below forms a plan that will help you record your online actions and keep you on track.

✼ In the first column, Action, record what tasks are most important to you right now. This could be 'tweeting'.

✼ Enter into the Benefits column what it is this action will do for you and your audience. For example, a benefit of tweeting that works well for both you and your audience is getting and giving feedback. You can use this feedback to find out how to improve your service and your followers can give you any praise or criticism.

✼ Then you can tick the Completed column when you have completed the task.

✼ Note in the Measurement column how you will measure the success of this action. With tweeting, you will gain more followers, get more hits on your website, and receive more feedback. If you are not sure about how Twitter can help your project, we will be looking at this in the later chapter dedicated to Twitter.

| Action | Benefits | | Completed | Measurement |
	To me	To my audience		

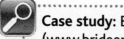

Case study: Bláithín O'Reilly Murphy, Bride Enomics (www.brideenomics.com)

Bláithín had been a wedding planner and worked in the wedding industry for nine years before starting this new venture. She recognized that over these years she'd made many mistakes in both business and marketing and could see other suppliers and professionals in that industry making those same costly mistakes. She knew that, like her, many of these professionals were great at what they did but it was the business side that was letting them down. With this in mind, she launched Bride Enomics to help others develop their marketing skills and ultimately 'book more brides'.

Bláithín has discovered that writing online can help boost these businesses; being a blogger herself and running several social media profiles, she's reaching a much larger audience and has gained several new contacts around the globe. When she was invited to speak at a conference in America, she used her online presence to strengthen her position and interact with attendees before and after the event.

With her own online writing and for others, she says, 'It all boils down to common sense. Keep it professional, courteous and kind. All of my clients are professionals but of course they have private lives, too. I do encourage people to share some of their "personal stories" online; it's good for clients to see you as a rounded individual, but at all times you want to keep it appropriate. It's fine to say you are enjoying a nice glass of wine or cocktail with friends, but it's a big no-no to say you are drunk and swinging from the chandelier!'

When working with other businesses, Bláithín helps them define their messages by pinpointing what they are trying to achieve (the product) and whom they want to achieve this with (the audience). She encourages them to keep their messages to the point, clear and concise. She knows that, through sharing her own personal experiences and ideas that have worked well for her, she has been able to build a much stronger relationship with her readers. By sharing her experience with other businesses, they can create their own strong online presence and ultimately 'book more brides'.

On delivering the message

Robert says...

I've worked for myself for more than 20 years now and don't really differentiate between my work and my home life. Clearly, I filter out from my business communication stuff that is very personal or of no relevance to my public persona, but, equally, I share more than most.

As a writer, I inevitably draw on personal experience, perception and prejudice. And the consultancy work I do requires emotional as well as intellectual engagement. So, just as a therapist gives a little of themselves to counter the client's quest, I, too, use all of myself to achieve results.

It's what you do if you have a public profile and what you never do if you are a senior corporate figure. In fact, rise to the top of your industry and the press will expose more of your private life than you will find comfortable.

My message is a personal one. I work in a very human way with people and organizations seeking to overcome vulnerability. We are all different. You need to get that work–life balance – right in your writing, too.

Jess says...

As Robert is both the business and the product, he can be more laid back and informal in delivering the message online – he needs to be himself as that is what people are buying. As Robert's employee and therefore a representative of him, all the messages I put online have to support his overall business message and retain a professional tone and style. My key message is therefore always selling Robert and any online communication aims to promote his skills, experience, projects and services to those who would be interested in finding out more and eventually hiring him. Everything I write has to be related to the business and can't cross over with my personal life.

Focus points

✳ There are three main reasons why people build their online presence: (1) getting enquiries, (2) strengthening relationships, and (3) building a brand or profile.

✳ Only target your online writing to those who will be most interested in what you have to say or sell.

✳ Your copywriting style needs to match the style of your brand and to be professional.

✳ Whatever a successful competitor is doing, you should be doing the same.

✳ Success can be measured in a number of ways and the best way will depend on what your project is – it may be online views, enquiries or comments.

Summary

You now better appreciate what your main motivation is for increasing and improving your online activity. The message you are trying to communicate will fall under one or more of the three categories we have covered: getting enquiries, strengthening relationships, or building a profile or brand.

You also now better understand the benefits of each of these and what the impact can be on your project. Everything that you put online will have your message subtly running behind it, encouraging people to do what it is you want, and will therefore take you closer to reaching your goal. Think about what you have learned in this chapter – are your motives right? Perhaps you have realized that there's more you can do to help your project than you first thought.

We have also begun preparing you as you take your first steps into writing for the Web and, having successfully profiled your audience and competitors, you have put together a list of action points that we will be working towards. As you progress through the book, don't be afraid to add more to your list as you learn new things – just don't overload yourself!

Next step

Do you remember us asking if you had a website? We will be looking at that in the next chapter. Don't worry if you haven't got one; we will talk you through setting one up – simply and cheaply!

Your website

In this chapter you will learn:

- ▶ *to crack the terminology used to describe websites and their features*
- ▶ *about the main types of website*
- ▶ *how to make sure a website is accessible and attracts a large number of 'quality' visitors*
- ▶ *how to set up a website cheaply and easily using WordPress*
- ▶ *about the main features that every website should have.*

Self-assessment: How is my website working for me?

Take a look at the diagnostic test below and, starting at the top, respond to the statements honestly – it will help you work out what direction you need to head in.

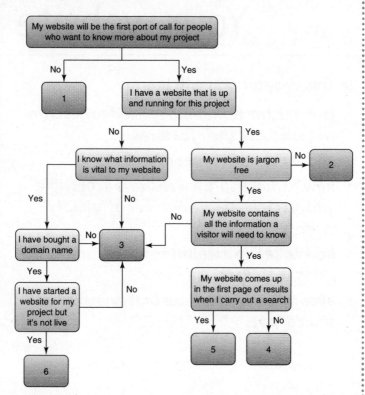

Feedback

1 Really? Your Web address can be put on adverts, business cards, email signatures and more. It will also be found in search engine listings. Bear in mind that the easiest way to access information is now on the Internet. Remember, almost everybody will look online first when searching for anything new. That's why you not only need to be there, but visible and clear too.

2 Take a look at what you have published on your website already. Does the jargon make it difficult to understand? Get a family member or friend with no connection to your project or line of work to read it through. If they have trouble understanding the content, you will probably need to revise it. You simply cannot assume that everyone you want to influence will understand the jargon you use. Your website should make sense to everyone – even journalists who might be researching a story. We will cover how to work around the jargon later in this chapter.

3 Don't worry, we will be covering all this below!

4 We will be looking at how your website can rise through the possible pages and pages of search results by making it 'search engine friendly' – this is called search engine optimization (SEO).

5 Good! But be sure to carry out both name searches and sector searches. We will be researching different keywords in this chapter to ensure that your website is showing up for the correct search terms. You will learn that it's not the quantity of website visits that counts, but the quality.

6 For some reason you have stopped progressing with your site and haven't 'gone live'. It may be that your website is missing the information it needs and you are not sure what to include. You may just not have time to finish it until now. Check out our quick and easy website set-up guide in case you find it easier than what you have already chosen and set up. Remember that a website should be a dynamic, living thing. It will never be perfect, but always a work in progress. Better to publish and continue to develop than to wait until you feel it is perfect and ready to go live.

Remember this: Sell yourself!

Your website homepage is your online point of sale – don't let it let you down! Investing your time and effort is extremely worth while if it helps you succeed. Remember, too, that it's vital to make your website personal. That means writing as if speaking directly to your audience.

Your shop window

'The role of a writer is not to say what we all can say, but what we are unable to say.'

Anaïs Nin

A website for your project can be very important. It will become a one-stop shop for all the information any virtual passer-by needs to know. More importantly, it becomes the place you put all the information you want them to know.

Your website, be it a personal site or one promoting an organization or project, is your shop window. You can put what you want on display, in the order you want. Then you can link to supporting material that enables your website visitor to dig deeper and find out more.

There are so many different styles of website that you may find your head spinning just thinking about it. How many pages should it have? Should you use video as well as images and text? Should you pay for a professional Web designer to make it look pretty? In this chapter we will take you through a really simple way of setting yourself up with a website – you can always build on it at a later date as your project develops, or you can shift the information to a new platform as and when you feel the need. We will also cover what information your site definitely needs to contain and how best to lay it out. Most importantly, we will show you how to write your website content effectively.

Terminology

Before we jump into different websites and getting one set up for your project, let's run through some of the phrases you may come across in this chapter as you set your site up. It's jargon that others use and we don't want you to get confused.

Cookie Also known as an HTTP cookie, this is a small piece of data that is sent from a website to your browser to be stored there. This helps websites monitor your previous visits and enables the website to 'remember' you. This can be very helpful in that you do not have to re-input your name and address on, for example, an e-commerce site that you have visited before. So-called tracking cookies are more controversial because they enable the website owner to understand and track your progress through their site. Nowadays you have to click to consent to a website placing cookies on your computer.

DNS – Domain Name System This translates your domain into an IP address.

IP Address – Internet Protocol Address This is a numerical label associated to a device connected a computer network, to help identify that device and its location.

Metadata These don't affect the display of the site but instead provide background information in the HTML/XHTML coding of a page, such as what the page is about it, who created it, when it was updated and so on. Search engines use this information when indexing HTML sites. The information contained in the meta-description tag will be what search engines display in search results when listing your site.

Nameserver(s) A server which controls the DNS for a domain, it allows you to decide which hosting company controls your web space and email.

SEO – Search Engine Optimization This is how 'search engine friendly' a website is – those with good SEO will appear higher on SERPs and those with poor SEO will never get a high natural ranking.

SERP – Search Engine Results Page This is simply the page of results you get when you search for a term or phrase using a search engine.

Site description This is the text that will be displayed under your site title in search engine results – search engines use this to get an idea of what your site is about.

Site title This will appear at the top of browser windows and tabs when someone is viewing your site. It's also how search engines will list you.

Spam These are unsolicited bulk messages that are usually advertising a product or service.

Widgets These are basically extra blocks you can add to your website. It may be that you want to display a photo or logo to the side of your content – there will be an image widget for that. You can also add a list of links – maybe to other sites that interest you, or projects that you support or that support you. (Widgets are easy to use and help you avoid getting involved with – or paying for – programming.)

Wireframe This is a road map of your site showing all the different routes a visitor can take through your pages.

XHTML/HTML/CSS Extensible HyperText Markup Language, HyperText Markup Language and Cascading Style Sheets are the languages that websites are written in to enable the information to be sent from server to server. If you are running your site through WordPress or similar, you won't need to worry too much about this. If you want to custom-design the look of your site, you will need a good working knowledge of CSS in order to do so (or find someone to help you who does).

Types of website

On your online journey you will visit many different websites that all do different things. The type of site that you need to set up will depend on the nature of your project. Most websites can be set up as 'content-managed' – this means that, while you may not have full access to edit and alter the look of your site, you can definitely edit the content, add images and keep it up to date.

E-COMMERCE

These sites are used solely to sell products or services. Your customers are able to make payments online and you can receive the money directly into your account. It was once common for people to pay to have code written especially in order for them to sell items online, but now sites such as PayPal, Amazon and eBay make it extremely easy for you to integrate online purchasing into your site.

Perfect for: selling.

BLOG

The best-known blog-hosting sites are WordPress and Blogger, both of which can handily also be used to set up as a main website. We will run you through this later in the chapter. Using these, you can quickly and easily post your own thoughts, ideas, news and commentary without hiring any third-party help.

Perfect for: sharing.

BROCHURE

This is literally a website that could have been a brochure. They both contain the same static text and images. Though some people may be happy with a brochure website, it is very much where Web marketing started a decade ago. Most have moved on to more sophisticated, interactive sites. Updated regularly with fresh content to keep people coming back to your site, it's an acceptable first step.

Perfect for: the basics.

Key idea: Content-managed websites

The best-qualified person to add new content to your website is you or, if not you, someone close to you and the work you do. The art of content management is to get a designer to help you create the best website framework, into which you can quickly and easily add content, links, news and opportunities.

You may recall a time when all website changes were made by specialist Web designers. Not only can this be costly, it is also slow. You need to add content to your website when it's right for you or a commercial opportunity.

Will my website work?

On a scale of effectiveness, that's a difficult question to answer. It depends mostly on what your project is and how well the site actually turns out. If you are offering a unique and niche service/product that you know there's a target market for, then yes, you should find yourself receiving quite a few website visits, providing your site is set up correctly.

If, however, you are simply one fish swimming in a sea of others, it becomes more difficult. It then becomes a question of 'How are you different from the others?'

That's a marketing question you may need to answer. In fact, your website should magnify the positive differences between you and your rivals. That way, even if you are actually all offering similar things, it becomes easier for people to choose between you.

Differentiation is something that the Internet lets you do well, but only if you fully understand what it means. You also need to be able to write in a way that illustrates how you differ from others.

People need choice to make a decision. That's why restaurants always do better when in close proximity to other restaurants. People like to walk along the street, browse menus, look through the window and then make their choice.

Your website is both that menu and window. It needs to say what you offer and illustrate what the experience will be like. Often what tips the balance in favour of one restaurant over another is quite small. Let's develop the analogy and see how it translates into your task of building a website.

Restaurant	Website
My favourite dish is on the menu	You have listed exactly what I'm looking for
Bread, olives and water are included in the price of a main course	Your price includes delivery; the others don't make this clear
I can see people enjoying themselves through the window	There are customer testimonials listed

The design brief

Regardless of whether you intend to start your website yourself or hire a professional designer, it's always important to have a written outline of how exactly you want your site to look and function. Here's a list of things you need to consider:

▶ **Type of site** How will a website benefit your project? What is its main aim? Is it simply to share information or attract a response? Will it be interactive, enabling people to add their own comments?

▶ **The purpose of the site** What do you want the website to do? The more accurately you can define this, the better your website will be. What do you want visitors to do when they visit your site? The purpose will define what content your pages need to have. Embedding a subtle 'call to action' on each page can be key to converting visitors into enquiries.

▶ **Look** Do you want your site to follow a corporate style, or reflect your personal tastes in colour, style and font?

▶ **Competition** What do your competitor's sites look like? You can't copy their style like for like, but perhaps they've incorporated a particular element that would work for you, too. Conversely, by being very different visually, you will differentiate your site from theirs. What information do they include? What offers are they running? Should you be doing the same and how can you be different?

▶ **Audience** Who do you envisage visiting your site? It must appeal to them and be easy to navigate or they will avoid using it.

▶ **Pages** What content do you want your site to have? How will the pages be linked and how will they appear on the site?

▶ **Extras** Does the site need more than basic text? It's always worth having images and video to make the site more dynamic. Which pages would these go on? Do you need a shopping cart? A newsletter sign-up feature? A diary?

- **Timings** Do you have a particular date by when you need your site up and running? Perhaps in time for a new product launch, or even for your business launching? Giving yourself a target date to 'go live' can help focus and motivate you – leave it open-ended and you may keep putting it off.

- **Accessibility** There are a number of protocols about how you make your site accessible to all. For example, your site should be accessible to a person with a visual impairment.

 Try it now: The design brief

Take the list above and write your own sections under each heading. Remember to include as much detail as possible. This will help you when it comes to putting your site together. Once you have finished, review and edit your brief. This is a good habit to get into – it's how professionals write!

The must-haves

There are several things that your website *must* contain. If it's missing this information, your online communication will suffer. Here are the most important things your website needs:

YOUR DOMAIN

This is the key piece of information and not as obvious as you might first think. Your domain could be:

- your own name, for example www.robertashton.co.uk

- derived from a likely search term such as www.worldsbestauthor.com

- describe what it is you are offering www.ghostwriteyourbook.com

Remember that the domain name, site description and the large text you place on your homepage could all be similar, or different. For example, Robert's own website, www.robertashton.co.uk, could have the site description 'world's best author' and on the homepage, 'Let me ghost-write your book'.

Actually, we don't make that bold claim about his writing and nor does he ghost-write books for others. If he did, then the rest of the site would need to explain the ghost-writing service and support the bold claim. Otherwise, it would lack credibility and people would not take any of it seriously.

CONTACT DETAILS

It's always best to include all different types of contact – email, telephone, and address. Although email is becoming the most used method of communication, this doesn't mean that everyone is using it.

Your address will be used when people want to write to you or post things out to you – if you work from home and don't want to use your personal address, you can currently arrange to use a Post Office Box for less than £25 a month. Telephone still remains the quickest way to get in touch with someone, and so, if someone needs some information from you quickly, then they will need a telephone number.

You would be surprised how many websites have typos in the phone number. Do make sure the number is typed correctly – a rogue digit can make the caller's life very difficult.

Remember that, although one benefit of a website is that it enables people the world over to contact you, they will want to know that you are based somewhere. Websites that give no indication of the location of the person or organization behind it can look 'dodgy'. Even if your site doesn't carry a postal address, do make it clear which city in the world is your closest and therefore an easily recognizable physical location.

WHAT YOU DO

Don't make this description long-winded – keep it as simple as possible. Put yourself in your visitor's shoes and think about the answers to these questions:

- ▶ What do you want them to know about you and your work?
- ▶ What do you want them to think will be the benefits of connecting with you?
- ▶ What do you want them to do – ring you, buy something or perhaps sign an e-petition?

Everything you write online should seek to answer these three questions.

KEYWORDS

We will be looking at these in more detail a little later on – these are specific words or phrases that you will need to use frequently on your site for search engines to scan, catalogue and refer to when helping people find your site.

Key idea: Keeping it fresh

Search engines like new content on websites. It shows that the site is still active and up to date, proving that your project is still running and worthy of a listing on a SERP. (Can you remember what this is? Check back to the beginning of this chapter if not.)

THINGS TO AVOID

Don't:

▸ **include what you are not on your website.** Search engines like Google will pick up keywords and therefore include your site in searches for those keywords. This means that you will get visitors to your site that are looking for what you are not. For example, you could write, 'We are not a consultancy or a drop-in centre.' The search engine will scan your site, pick up *consultancy* and *drop-in centre* and then list you for those results.

▸ **criticize other projects and people.** No matter what negative experience you have dealing with other companies, projects or people, never complain about them online. It's extremely unprofessional and should be carried out through the official channels if necessary.

▸ **be boring!** Keep your text lively, informative and interesting. People will shut off if they aren't interested in what they are reading. It's a key difference between books and websites. People expect fewer words and more pictures. They simply will not read lengthy passages of text.

▸ **use jargon.** If your visitors aren't likely to understand a word or phrase, don't use it. You want to make your text as easy to read as possible – by as many people as possible. If people don't understand what you are trying to say, they will feel alienated and be less likely to approach you. If there's a specific term or phrase that is vital to what you do, you should perhaps include a definition of that word somewhere prominent so people can understand.

Getting visitors

Aside from marketing your website by including it on your business cards, Facebook profile and so on, you should also think about the following.

SEARCH ENGINE OPTIMIZATION

The better your site's SEO, the easier it will be for search engines to list you in results and give you a higher position on a SERP (Search Engine Results Page).

Even better, good SEO is a free way to get yourself these higher positions. Search engines scan your site and pick up keywords, which is why it's so important to list only what you are and not what you are not. Search engines are sophisticated, for sure, but also very easily confused. You need to make sure that search engines include your site in relevant searches, to ensure that you are getting the right traffic to your site.

It's all very well getting plenty of hits, but it's the *quality* of those hits that counts. As the Internet has become the main source of all information, the need to have good SEO has become paramount.

There are lots of companies now offering to improve your website's SEO. They understand keywords and will also use Google Analytics to see which words your potential customers are using most often in their online searches. To understand how Google can help you choose the best keywords, check out Google AdWords. You don't have to place an ad; just see the relative popularity of the keywords you are thinking of using.

Many website design companies now include good SEO as part of the site's design; they know that metadata affects how search engines find your website.

🔑 Key idea: Become search-engine friendly

Increased search engine friendliness = more site visitors = more prospective clients = more leads generated = more contacts/sales made. It's a win-win situation – search engines can see what you are offering to people through keywords and can tell you are trusted through inbound links – you therefore get a higher position on SERPs and more site visitors.

🕐 Try it now: Pinpoint your keywords

Take a piece of paper and write a list of the terms you would use when describing your project. It might be services you provide or a specific target audience. Make sure they are relevant and really apply – don't list words that are only marginally applicable. Bear in mind that you want only high-quality traffic – getting people to visit your site who aren't really interested won't do your project any favours. For example, for Robert's site we include the following keywords:

Barefoot entrepreneur	Conference facilitator
Big society support	Business start-up support
Business consultancy	Keynote speaker
Robert Ashton	Growing a business
Business author	

When you have got your list, you ideally need to refine it to 15 terms or fewer. The more specific you can be the better. You will then need to make sure you include these words somewhere in the main content of your site, repeatedly if possible. We will be thinking about these when we start writing your content later in the chapter.

🧠 Remember this: Keywords

Keywords are extremely important. If you aren't marketing your site in any other way but simply relying on people finding you on search engines, keywords are the be-all and end-all of your website. You therefore need to make sure that you have your keywords down to a very specific list and that you use them whenever you can.

MAKING YOUR SITE SEARCH ENGINE FRIENDLY

There are various things you need to think about when setting out your content. The most important of these, however, is to try to get it right first time. That means, as has already been said, writing clear, concise copy that is easy to understand and contains the keywords and phrases your audience will quite literally be searching for.

It really is very important to make your site as search engine friendly as possible. You need to be using your keywords as often as possible in the following positions:

- page titles

- page descriptions

- URLs (domain names)

- page content.

Don't force a keyword into one of the above if it actually isn't relevant – it will confuse visitors to your site if the content isn't actually about the keyword you have used.

A few years ago there was a trend to add lots of keywords in text the same colour as the background. The idea was that this would be hidden from the viewer but visible to search engines. Some unscrupulous people even used to list rival business names and product names in the hope of attracting people looking for them. We are pleased to say that this technique no longer works. Google, in particular, is now far too sophisticated to be so easily fooled.

INBOUND LINKS

Another factor that increases the quality of your SEO is inbound links. These are links from other websites to your own site and are also known as backlinks. While some companies offer paid backlinks, avoid these at all costs because they won't actually improve your site's SEO. This is because search engines now have software that can detect a paid-for or irrelevant inbound link. Plus, they make your site look tacky if you are required to link back to the site you have bought the link from.

The reason search engines like backlinks is because they show that other sites think you are a worthwhile source to link to, increasing your site's validity and authority. The best way to get links back to your website is by generating high-quality content that people will find interesting and useful. You can submit this content to higher-ranking sites and, if they use your piece, they will then link back to your site when crediting you as the author of the article.

Alternatively, you can start a blog on your site (really easy with WordPress). Use correct and appropriate keywords and Google will index these blog pages, allowing other people to find your articles and link to them off their own sites.

Other ways to generate links back to your website are to:

▶ comment on other people's relevant blogs, as these usually list your Web address

▶ comment on relevant news stories on media websites

▶ take part in discussions in Web forums and on LinkedIn.

A top tip is to include a hyperlink back from the comment to a relevant page of your website. This page should carry information that will be of interest, perhaps an article you have written. It should not link directly to your own online shop!

GOOGLE ADWORDS

This service is a paid-for way of getting a higher ranking in Google's search result pages. It does not, however, guarantee a position at the top of the page. If you take a look at a search results page, such as the one shown in Figure 3.1, you will see a shaded box at the top of the page and a strip of ads down the right-hand side – these are paid-for listings.

They are shown when the keywords you have used in your search match the keywords the advertiser has selected their advert to be shown for. Research shows that more people are likely to ignore these adverts and continue further down the page to find a naturally ranking result. While AdWords can get you a better SERP position, most people will know that you have paid to be there.

As we have briefly mentioned, AdWords is a very keyword-focused tool, with the ads that get displayed being dependent on the search terms used. If you decide to set up an AdWord listing, it's very important that you have that list of specific keywords you put together earlier. You will be able to expand on these by adding locations, but you will need to stick to the root of your project in order to create an effective AdWords campaign.

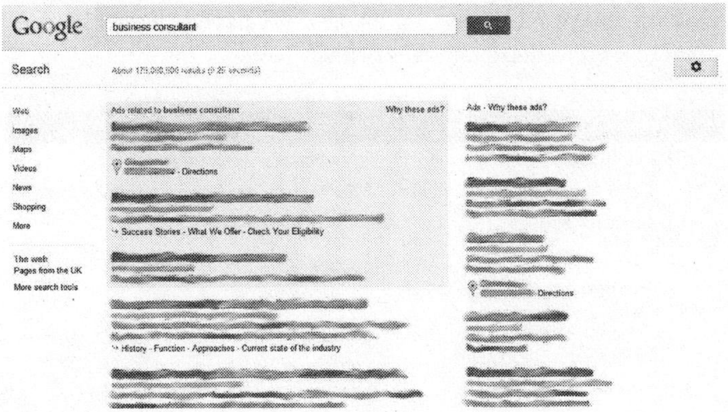

Figure 3.1 Sample Google search results page

A quick and easy website

We are using WordPress for this example, as, at the time of writing, it's one of the easiest, cheapest and best-known options, in our view. It's first and foremost a blogging platform, but goes further. It enables you to personalize your blog to the extent that it has all the same basic functionalities of a simple website. Before starting, though, you should make sure that you own, or are able to buy, the domain you want to use for the site. If you don't own it, head over to a domain-buying site such as Go Daddy, search for the domain and see if it's available to buy. If it's already been bought by someone else, you won't be able to use it and should try an alternative. If it is available to buy, then, great, go ahead. You will then be taken through the process of buying the domain and will be able to change the name servers when it comes to making your site 'go live'.

.COM VS. .ORG

WordPress has two different types of site that you can use to set up your website or blog. The most important difference between the two is that a wordpress.org site is self-hosted. This means that, while you have more control over the look and feel of your site, it is a bit more in-depth and you have to arrange your own hosting. You will need more than just a basic technical knowledge to run a wordpress.org site. By contrast, a wordpress.com site takes care of all the hosting and back-up and provides custom themes. We have summed up the advantages and disadvantages of each below.

	Advantages	Disadvantages
.com	Free and easy	Can't upload custom themes
	Technical maintenance is covered	Can't modify the PHP code behind the site
	Automatic back-up	Can't upload plug-ins
	Secure dashboard log-in	
	Search feature allows you to find like-minded bloggers	
.org	Can upload custom themes	Needs a good Web host
	Can upload plug-ins	Requires more technical knowledge
	Ability to change coding completely	No spam block automatically included
		No automatic back-ups
		No automatic updates to WordPress software

We recommend setting up your site with wordpress.com: there is less for you to worry about and, once you have found your way around, it is very easy to navigate and use.

GETTING STARTED

▶ **Step 1**

Head over to www.wordpress.com and click 'Sign up free' or 'Get started here'.

▶ **Step 2**

Choose a blog address. It's a good idea to keep it similar to the website domain you have bought. Once you register the domain to the site, you won't see the blog address you have chosen.

▶ Step 3

Pick a username and password. WordPress will automatically take your blog name and make your username the same but you can change this. The username will appear when you publish comments and 'posts'. You will need a valid email address when you register – WordPress will send a confirmation email to this email address in order for you to confirm that you want to set up an account. You won't be able to use an email address that already has a WordPress account linked to it. If you already have a WordPress account, you can easily add a new blog site to that account.

▶ Step 4

Check that the language setting is correct and hit 'Create blog' under the free version (you can upgrade later if you want). You will then need to head over to the email account you used to sign up to WordPress and click the activation link in the email that WordPress will have sent. Once you have activated your blog, you will get a second email confirming that from WordPress.

▶ Step 5

When you click the activation link in your email from WordPress, you will be taken directly to a page where you will be asked to choose a theme. This is basically how your site will look. There are lots to choose from – some are free and some are 'premium', which you have to pay for. You can change the theme of your site whenever you like, so you will not be stuck with whichever one you begin with.

▶ Step 6

After picking your theme or choosing to stick with the default, you will be taken to your dashboard. This is where you can access every bit of your site; you can accept comments, add new content, rearrange menus, change your theme, and more. It will look very similar to Figure 3.2.

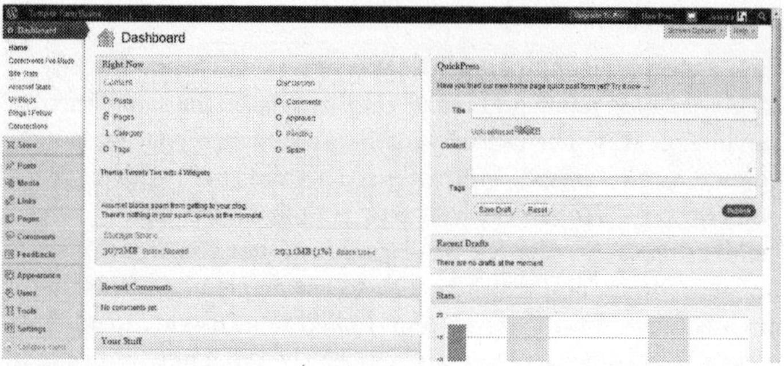

Figure 3.2 Basic dashboard on www.wordpress.com

You will start off with one default page, post and comment that you can edit or delete. The menu on the left is really easy to navigate and pretty self-explanatory:

▶ **Posts** These will be the blog-style articles that you can use to update news and special offers. You will set all these to appear under one **page** and they will appear in reverse chronological order, so the most recent posts will always appear at the top. **Sticky posts** will always appear at the top of the page above regular posts. You can use **categories** and **tags** to group these and make them easier to find by topic.

▶ **Page** These will be your main static articles. These will appear all the time in either a header menu, if your theme allows one, or a sidebar menu (to the left or right of your page).

You can return to the dashboard at any point by hovering over your username in either the top right or left of the screen and selecting 'Dashboard' from the drop-down options. If you have more than one blog registered to your WordPress account, you will be able to access the other dashboards by hovering over the right-hand menu and then highlighting the blog and selecting the 'Dashboard' option from the menu that appears.

For further tips on how to add and edit pages and add media, visit www.learn.wordpress.com. If you get stuck at any point, there's a really good support site at www.en.support.wordpress.com, and if you can't find the answer you are looking for, the WordPress community can help on their forum. Post your queries and issues on www.en.forum.wordpress.com.

Figure 3.3 WordPress.com page with Dashboard drop-down menu

Remember this: Content hierarchy

Organize the content on your website so that the most important information for your reader can be found at the top of the page. Any additional content should then flow down the page in order of importance. Your visitors need to be able to find the most vital information quickly, and not waste their time trawling your site trying to find it.

Main pages and features

YOUR HOMEPAGE

This is likely to be your most visited page. It is the page that will come up when people enter your domain name straight into their browser. It's also likely to be the first page people see if they have searched for your project name. If it's plain with no colour and very few words, visitors won't feel encouraged to take a further look around your site.

It's important that this first view of your site is welcoming and inviting. This is also the page that people will revert back to from the various different areas or pages of your site, so it must be easily accessible. Most people use this page to provide a brief 'welcome' to the site and the project, giving a quick summary of what it is you do and what a visitor will be able to find on the site. In short, they should have some good reasons to explore further!

As it's possibly the most-viewed page, whatever you want people to see should be visible somewhere on this page. It might be that call to action we mentioned earlier – what you want people to do when they visit your site. Any special offers should be clearly marked on the homepage, prominently so that this particular area draws the visitor's attention. You also need to make it easy for the visitor to go from this page to the other main pages of your site.

ABOUT

This page will go into more detail about what you or your project are all about. It's what you do, who you do it for, and who's behind it. Here you can highlight any aims or goals that your project has – if your visitors sympathize with these, they are more likely to work with you.

If your project has a team of people working behind it, it's always nice for visitors to see who they are. If you have got a large team, don't list everyone – just those in senior or customer-facing positions. Include a head-and-shoulders image of each person, their name, position (e.g. Chief Executive Officer, Head of Sales, Marketing Manager) and a brief biography. How long have they been working for the project? What is their experience in that sector? What jobs do they deal with? Make these notes light and personal, not stuffy and boring.

It can also be handy to include specific emails for each person or department, to ensure that queries can be directed to the right area. A generic info@yourdomainname doesn't reassure your visitors that their query is going to be handled by the correct person.

CONTACT

Here you need to list all the details we mentioned before: telephone numbers (for each department if necessary), postal address and email addresses (again, for each person/department or just a generic address).

To prevent spam, some people prefer to use a contact form on their websites instead of making email addresses public. However, these can simply form another barrier, preventing spontaneous contact. If the user clicks on an email address on a webpage, it usually opens their email program. It's then simply a matter of adding a message and clicking 'send'.

If you would like to use your email address but are worried about spam, instead of typing info@yourdomainname you can write it out slightly differently – info[AT]yourdomainname – giving a brief instruction to visitors who wish to contact you to remove the bracketed part and replace with the @ symbol. However, this can also inhibit people from contacting you. It's preferable to be easy to contact and invest in a good anti-spam application to filter out junk emails.

It's also worth ensuring that an email address or telephone number is visible from any page, so include it in the footer of the site in an additional widget. This means that, if anyone has any queries when viewing a page, they can immediately pick up the phone or write an email to find out more.

PRODUCT PAGES OR SHOP

If you are trying to sell a service or product, you need to give details. This doesn't necessarily mean that you have to take online payments – that's optional, although desirable. But do tell visitors how they can buy your products/services if you don't take online payments. Even an order form people can download, print, complete and post is better than nothing.

If your site mainly serves to list your products, you may find it easier to list them by category. You can give each category its own page, with the individual products in that category listed on those pages.

For example, someone selling jewellery would have different pages for bracelets, necklaces and rings, with each product then listed on those pages. If, on the other hand, you have a small product range, you may decide to have one page about your products and then detail how these can be bought.

If you do offer a service but you don't charge for it, let visitors know how they can book or find out more. Remember that on each page you want your visitors to either buy or find out more, so make this really easy for them to do. In fact, this is a good tip for anything you write online. Always offer people two options – of which neither is 'no'. That way you will get a higher response rate. For example:

- ▶ Click *here* to download our catalogue or *here* to request a copy by post.

- ▶ Sign up *here* for our monthly newsletter or *here* for our weekly service bulletins.

Include online payment buttons or a link to email you to get in touch. While one person might prefer to pay online, another may wish to pay by cheque. If you allow these different forms of payment, then make it clear that they have these options. Include a brief product description with each item, a photo if applicable and a price. Then add payment buttons next to each item, if you are using PayPal.

If you have lots of items to sell, it might be best to look into getting an e-commerce site set up for you, whose main purpose will be to take online payments.

PRICING AND SHIPPING

Make this clear – you want to avoid any payment mistakes. Also indicate what currency your items are priced in. Just putting 'Price: 5.00' next to an item won't help anyone – use currency symbols! Also, let people know how much you charge for postage and packaging and if you distribute internationally or which areas you serve. If it's difficult for you to pin down a specific price for an item because the cost depends on various factors, then include a range: give a minimum and maximum value. This way, your visitors won't be in for a shock if they enquire further.

BLOG

This can be vital in getting recurring visitors to your site. Keep people coming back for more, with the promise of interesting new content – and meet that promise! You can use your blog to announce project news or simply to share your thoughts and commentary on relevant matters. Don't forget that search engines love to know your site is active! Regular blogs will help with this. See Chapter 8 to learn how to write a blog.

SEARCH

This box is usually coded into your site so it appears at a constant fixed position, viewable from every page on your site. In WordPress, there's a Search widget you can add to the header, side or footer of your site. This feature makes it easy for people to find specific articles – another example of where your keywords and tags come in handy.

Other pages

The pages and features that we have covered above are those you should definitely include on your site. The ones below will apply to some projects, but not all. Think about the benefits they could have on your site and how easy they'd be for you to set up and manage.

TESTIMONIALS/REVIEWS

Even if you are just starting out, you can have testimonials on your website. All you have to do is ask people who know you and value what you do to provide one.

Testimonials should be short, direct and written using everyday language. There's nothing wrong with asking everyone you do business with for a testimonial. Many people even suggest what those testimonials might contain.

For example, you might write:

> 'Thank you for attending our recent course on decluttering your home. I hope we left you motivated to actually do some sorting out. Rachel, the trainer who worked with you, said you were particularly impressed with our 'seven steps to an organized kitchen'. Would you be willing to provide a testimonial for our website? It would be hugely encouraging to others as well as publicly recognizing your achievement.

> 'Something like: "Unpacking my shopping so that I put the new cans at the back, not the front of the cupboard, is a really simple idea. It means I always use the oldest cans first and no longer find myself throwing away out-of-date food.

This was just one of the money-saving tips I picked up on your course.' Lynn Packard, Chester."

The easier you make it for people to provide testimonials, the more testimonials you will collect. It really is that simple.

You can set testimonials out like this:

'Testimonial text here.'

Mr Bob, Bob Enterprises, www.companywebsite.co.uk

If the testimonial comes from an individual, put their name and location, as in the Lynn Packard example above.

If you receive reviews about specific products or services, rather than your project in general, add the most impressive one first, with others underneath. There's no reason why you shouldn't place testimonials throughout your website. The best place is next to the product or service to which they refer.

Whenever you finish some work for a client, or distribute a product, send out an email asking for feedback by default. This allows anyone to issue their feedback, but lets them keep it short. Check out www.surveymonkey.com for survey sending options. Satisfaction surveys can be really useful in collecting statistical data. For example, '85 per cent of those completing this survey agree that badgers should not be culled' would be a useful point to make on your website if you run a campaign to protect badgers.

PRESS AND MEDIA MENTIONS

Again, if you are just starting out, there may not be too many of these kicking around. When your business launched, did the local media cover it? Link back to any articles that mention you positively and also include links to any blogs that might quote or mention you. If you don't think you are ever likely to attract enough media attention to warrant a whole page dedicated to press, then perhaps just create a new blog/news article whenever there is the odd mention of you in the media. Make sure the articles contain links to your website. This will help your search engine rankings.

FREQUENTLY ASKED QUESTIONS (FAQS)

This can literally be a page of common questions you find yourself being asked about your project. Answering FAQs in this way can save you going into too much detail about them on other pages.

Importantly, FAQs can also pose the questions to which you want people to have answers. In other words, once you know the most likely reasons people give for not buying from you, or signing up to your campaign, you can confront them head on in your FAQ pages.

For example, let's say your website promotes a music festival. At last year's event you had a problem with security and a few people had things stolen from their tents. You know this is likely to put people off booking again. You meet this with a very direct FAQ such as:

> **Q:** I'm worried about security – if I leave things in my tent, will they get stolen?
>
> **A:** We have dramatically improved our security this year. We will have twice the number of security staff patrolling the tent village as we had last year. We have also introduced 'Fort Knox', a marquee with coin-operated lockers that's manned 24/7 throughout the festival.

Checking and editing

Check that visitors can easily access the main pages and vital information. Make sure they can still manage to find their way back to the main pages from subsections. Then draft the initial content for each page. Don't forget that you can draft the content offline first, for a friend or colleague to check. If you are using WordPress, you can easily copy and paste into the page editor straight from your publishing program. Alternatively, you can work straight from the page editor but keep the articles as drafts, rather than making them public, until you are happy with the text. Use 'Preview' buttons to see your content as-is before publishing – you can then edit the text before making it public.

Try it now: Make your own wireframe

Look at the different pages we have discussed above. Think about which ones your site needs, then draw out a wireframe like the one in Figure 3.4 to show how the navigation on your site will work.

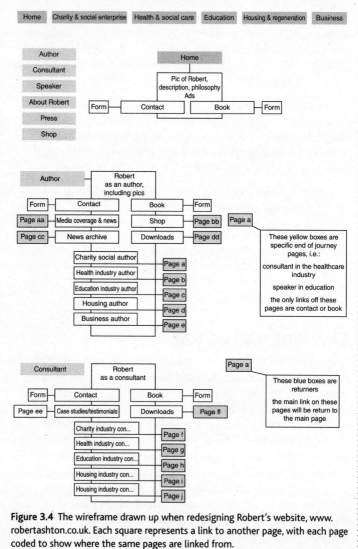

Figure 3.4 The wireframe drawn up when redesigning Robert's website, www. robertashton.co.uk. Each square represents a link to another page, with each page coded to show where the same pages are linked from.

Hyperlinks

Hyperlinks can be great for introducing another level to your content that readers can use for finding further information.

When linking to a website that is external to yours, it's always a good idea to set the hyperlink so that it opens in a new window. This will mean that visitors still have your website open and aren't immediately taken away from it.

Don't think that every other word needs to be a hyperlink – these must be relevant and necessary. If you think that the reader would like to know about a certain topic, organization or person mentioned in your text, insert a link to a website where they can click through to find out more; it might even be a different page on your own site.

Avoid using phrases such as 'Click here to read more'. Try to embed a hyperlink within a sentence that hasn't been written purely to introduce the hyperlink. Keep the linked text brief and don't try to explain it. Always double-check that the link you have created actually works.

For example, compare these two paragraphs:

> If you are in *housing* and *regeneration*, Robert can offer various services. *Click here* to find out more about speaking, *here* to find out about writing, or *here* to find out about consultancy.

> Robert offers various *speaking*, *writing* and *consultancy* services to those working in housing and regeneration.

In the first sentence, the words 'housing' and 'regeneration' didn't need to be links – if those terms applied to the reader, they would know what the words meant. If the terms didn't apply to the reader, they wouldn't be interested in finding out more. The second paragraph has eliminated the unnecessary words and kept the sentence short and simple.

Case study: R & B Catering (www.griddlechef.com)

Roger and Belinda knew that the world was heading online and they needed to be there themselves or lose out. It was pure coincidence that they met someone who was able to set them up with a simple one-page website with their own domain pointing at it for a one-off fee (Figure 3.5). The problem was that, although they could now be listed in search engine results, the website itself wasn't actually that good. They weren't happy with the text or images and became frustrated that they weren't able to make these edits themselves and had to rely on someone else to do it for them.

Figure 3.5 The site Roger and Belinda paid for but were unable to edit themselves. They hated the blurry background and how the text was presented.

They headed on over to wordpress.com and set themselves up with a new website, registered to the .com version of their other domain

(Figure 3.6). They have now been able to include the text, pages and images that they want and also plan to incorporate a blog. Roger will use this to update and showcase his amateur photographs of the 22 cows they keep at home. As the site is set up in WordPress, Roger and Belinda can change the site whenever they want and the soon-to-be-added blog means there will be an additional interest for site visitors to look at.

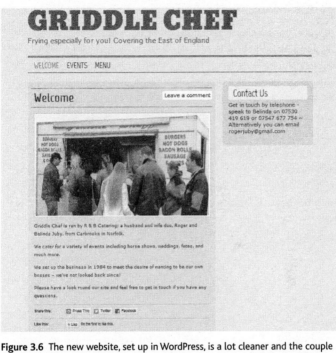

Figure 3.6 The new website, set up in WordPress, is a lot cleaner and the couple can add new content whenever they want. It will also cost them less to run as there is no longer a third party involved. Note, too, that people have the opportunity to share the site on Facebook and Twitter.

On websites

Robert says...

When I started my career we didn't have the Internet. This may sound insignificant, but actually things then were very different. Awareness was raised by advertising and reputation. Business information was printed and posted. Everything took longer and it was impossible to react quickly to changing conditions.

Today my website is my shop window, my CV, my diary and my notebook. Content has to be good, relevant and, especially, up to date. If I do not remove an event the day after it takes place, people will assume that everything is out of date.

My Twitter feed appears on my homepage. This means that minute by minute, new information, comment and links can be added. My iPad enables me to add this content wherever I am, whatever I am doing, with photos the instant it happens. Even my iPad is instantly available the moment I open the lid. It's faster than a laptop and, to me, still utterly captivating.

Of course, it's easy to believe that, if you are not constantly adding new content, blogging, tweeting or otherwise sharing, you are falling out of favour. This compulsion to be active online can be detrimental to your health. But, luckily, I can remember when none of this was possible and know that, while your Web presence is important, it is not a substitute for real life. You have to generate the content before you can add it!

Jess says...

Robert's main website is a content-managed site that is hosted by SubHub (www.subhub.com). It works well because our focus is on the textual content of the site and not so much about its functionalities. SubHub handles the technical side of things, so we don't have to worry about it. The CMS site suits our needs as I'm able to add new content immediately when needed, rather than waiting for someone else to have time to do it. When a change of design is needed, a complete design brief must be put together like the one we discussed earlier on in this chapter.

For Robert's side projects I use WordPress for setting up individual websites. I can then set these up myself without needing third-party help or advice. WordPress offers such a variety of free themes to use that it's very easy to find one that suits.

Focus points

* Your website is your online, and most influential, point of sale – make sure it's up to date and refreshed when possible.

* Ensure that your site is search engine friendly by reusing the most relevant keywords in your text.

* Avoid the use of jargon if your audience is unlikely to understand – keep your text as simple as possible but make it compelling with subtle calls to action.

* Check over your content before it 'goes live' and can be viewed by the public – get a friend to double-check if you are concerned about missing something yourself. They can let you know if they understand what you have written or if they feel you have missed anything vital from their external point of view. Bear in mind that, if your website is in the public domain, everything you have written is public – including your mistakes!

* Although having a website is essential, you need to actively support it, by writing new content to interest other sites and encourage inbound links and by having it in your email signature and on business cards.

Summary

In this chapter you have learned about the different types of website and what they can do. You will have chosen the best type of site for your project and may have started (or finished!) setting up your own. You know what pages you will want to include and what information needs to be on them. We have also looked at what you need to avoid doing so as not to alienate your site visitors, ensuring that your content is easy to read. You will now also understand how important it is to make your site search engine friendly and how this will increase the number of visitors to your site.

Remember that with a WordPress site you are in complete control of your content. If you are not happy with the look of your site but don't know any CSS, try a different theme or widgets in different places to change its appearance. Alternatively, you can look into getting a website designer to build you a WordPress site from scratch. They will design it for you but you will still be able to have full control over content.

Next step

We will be moving on to looking at how you can promote your project and site through social media. We will show you what you need to be saying, and how. First, though, we will take a look at social media in general.

Social media

In this chapter you will learn:

▶ *about the main social media platforms*

▶ *the importance of keeping your social media sites up to date and as fresh as possible*

▶ *about posting and responding to posts*

▶ *how to interlink between social media using a third-party service, such as TweetDeck or HootSuite.*

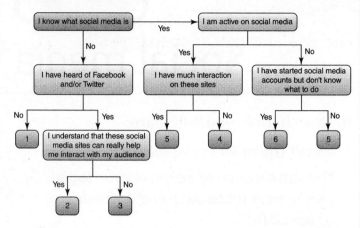

Self-assessment: How active are you on social media?

Look at the flow chart and answer the prompts honestly. Then read the relevant feedback below.

Feedback

1 Don't worry about not knowing a great deal about social media. The rest of this book will help you learn all you need to know. We give a brief overview of the most popular social media in this chapter and then go into more detail about Facebook, Twitter and LinkedIn in further chapters.

2 It might be that you haven't had time to set yourself up with social media accounts or haven't known where to start. We will cover the most important social media sites that you need be on – Facebook and Twitter.

3 We will cover the benefits of getting your project on to these sites in this chapter.

4 You may not be posting the right content or may simply not have enough time to update accounts. We will discuss the various types of updates that you can post and we will also look at delegating your social media activity.

5 Perfect! Do check out what type of content you should be posting in case there's something you are missing that will increase your level of interaction even further.

6 Don't worry – in the next two chapters we will be taking you through the main two social media sites, Facebook and Twitter, and teaching you how to use them.

The rise and rise of social media

'Right now, with social networks and other tools on the Internet, all of these 500 million people have a way to say what they are thinking and have their voice heard.'

Mark Zuckerberg, Facebook co-founder

Social media as a whole isn't new – it's been around for a good decade or so. But the landscape is changing frequently – a new site will become popular, then fade away as another site overtakes it in terms of functionality and popularity. The sites are constantly evolving to meet people's needs. However, some – such as Facebook and Twitter – are clearly here to stay. Others will be popular today and forgotten tomorrow.

Bebo, for example, was huge for connecting with your friends and acquaintances but now there's Facebook for that. MySpace is great for people trying to break on to the music scene but its user base has slowly declined. SoundCloud lets you share your own music; YouTube lets you share your own videos; Photobucket lets you share your own photos, and so on.

With more and more people owning smartphones, access to social media sites is even easier. You install the appropriate application on your phone and, hey presto, you can update your status, post videos and listen to music whenever and wherever you are.

In 2011, 91 per cent of all 16- to 24-year-olds and 76 per cent of 25- to 34-year-olds in the UK were using the Internet for social networking. Fifty-seven per cent of all UK Internet users used it for social networking purposes.

But social media is not just for the under-35s. Plenty of older people use social media websites, too. In fact, many grandparents use sites such as Facebook to keep in touch with family members around the world. The 2012 ONS report on Internet access showed that, between 2006 and 2012, the number of people aged 65-plus who had used a computer in the three months before the survey had doubled, from 23 to 46 per cent. Back in 2006, 9 per cent of those aged 65 and over who had used a computer within the previous three months had used a computer daily. By 2012 this had increased to 29 per cent. Interestingly, the 2012 results show that 96 per cent of those surveyed who fitted into the age groups 16–24 and 25–44 had used a computer in the previous three months, compared to 88 per cent and 84 per cent respectively in 2006.

Professionally, Twitter has become virtually indispensable as a way of keeping in touch with colleagues and customers. And LinkedIn, with its many special-interest groups and forums, while less dynamic, is certainly no less important.

Try it now: Your current knowledge

It might be that you are already very active on some social media sites... or maybe you have never signed up to one. Start by listing the different sites you know to be social networking sites. Then write a sentence about how each works. If you struggle with this task, don't worry – it's to help you find those grey areas that may need extra attention as you progress through this chapter.

What makes a social network?

If it's online and lets you connect and share with other like-minded people, then it's a social network. They allow you to network socially, but online. The biggest benefit is that by removing geography from the networking equation you can connect with people all over the world. In fact, one of the greatest feats is that you can extend your network to places you will never visit and connect with people you would never otherwise encounter.

The most popular social networking sites currently are Facebook and Twitter. We have devoted whole chapters to each of these two current social media giants. If you want to be successful online, you must become proficient with at least one and ideally both of these sites.

Here's a brief look at some other social networking sites that are rising and declining.

LINKEDIN
When: Launched May 2003

What: A social networking site for professionals. It allows you to connect with colleagues past and present and others you have met professionally. The site allows you to post recommendations for people you are connected to. These are very much like CV references and today, arguably, carry more weight. The site is popular among those looking for new work as current job vacancies are often advertised on company profiles. It is used extensively by recruitment consultants and headhunters. It reached 4 million UK users in June 2010.

Current status: By June 2012 it had a reported 175 million global users, with an increase of two new users every second.

MYSPACE
When: Launched in 2003

What: Based on the early social networking features of the site Friendster. From 2005 until early 2008 Myspace was the most visited social networking site in the world before Facebook overtook it. Past owners of the site include News Corporation, which in 2006 launched the site in the UK, mostly for music and entertainment users.

Current status: Currently owned by singer Justin Timberlake and Specific Media Group, who co-purchased the site in 2011. Despite several redesigns, the number of users is still on the decline. As of June 2012 the site had 25 million users and calls itself 'social entertainment'.

BEBO

When: Founded in 2005

What: 'Blog Early, Blog Often'. AOL bought the site off the founders in March 2008 for $850 million. The purchase coincided with the economic downturn and AOL felt unable to invest time and money into the site for it to compete with Facebook. AOL finally sold it off for reportedly less than $10 million to its current owners, Criterion Capital Partners. At the height of its popularity, its number of unique users (10.7 million) overtook that of Myspace.

Current status: The site was redesigned in 2011 following its most recent sale and has had a new notification feature added (similar to that of Facebook). In early 2012 the site crashed, which led users to believe it had closed for good, but Criterion Capital Partners claimed the new features they were trying to instal had caused the site to crash. It's currently very popular among role-players.

PINTEREST

When: Launched March 2010

What: Users 'pin' content of interest to share with others. The majority of content is image-based, so it isn't for everyone. Certainly, businesses related to design, food, beauty and lifestyle could find it useful.

Current status: In January 2012 it was reported that Pinterest had become the fastest site to break the 10 million unique visitors barrier with more than 11 million users. The majority of its users are female. According to Experian Hitwise, the site became the third largest social network in the United States in March 2012, rising above LinkedIn. There has been some controversy involving copyright laws, because images are being 'pinned' and shared without permission of their owner.

TUMBLR
When: Launched April 2007

What: A micro-blogging site that within two weeks of its launch had gained 75,000 users. It was the first blogging platform to host a blog for Barack Obama and is known for the viral blog 'We are the 99%', now the slogan of the Occupy Wall Street movement.

Current status: As of 18 July 2012, Tumblr has over 64.7 million blogs, with more than half of its visitors aged under 25.

SOUNDCLOUD
When: Launched October 2008

What: A social networking site purely for uploading, sharing and promoting audio recordings. It was a strong competitor with Myspace as it allowed recording artists to interact more freely and easily with others. In 2010 the site hit the 1 million users mark. It went on to reach 5 million users a year later.

Current status: In January 2012 SoundCloud announced that it had 10 million users. The platform can be integrated with both Facebook and Twitter accounts to allow seamless promotion across platforms of newly uploaded music files.

YOUTUBE
When: Launched November 2005

What: A platform allowing users to upload and share their own video files. The first video to be uploaded was titled 'Me at the zoo' and shows one of the site's co-founders at San Diego Zoo. In 2006 it claimed to have 65,000 new videos uploaded every day.

Current status: It now operates as a subsidiary of Google after being bought in November 2006 for $1.65 billion. It is ranked as the third most visited site behind Google and Facebook. In 2012 YouTube stated that the site was streaming 4 billion videos per day. It's been possible to upload 3D videos on the site since 2009 and, with the ever-increasing number of films and television shows now available in 3D, it is probable that that there will be a significant increase in the number uploaded to YouTube.

PHOTOBUCKET

When: Founded and launched in 2003

What: An image-hosting site that can be used to share photos and create slideshows. It also offers video hosting but limitations apply to users with free accounts. Like Myspace, News Corporation gained some control over the site after Fox Media International bought it in 2007.

Current status: It was announced in 2011 that Photobucket had become the default sharing platform for Twitter users. As with Pinterest, there has been some controversy over images being shared without prior consent from those that hold the copyright.

Key idea: Learning the lingo

All these sites above have their own different features and services. What's called one thing on one site will be called something completely different on the other. Don't worry if it all seems confusing to begin with – we list some of the important phrases for Twitter and Facebook in the following chapters – because you will pick them up as you progress with updating your profiles and getting to grips with how to use the different sites. If you have no experience with social media at all, don't expect to run before you can walk. Simply take one step at a time.

The art of conversation

You may find that, especially in larger businesses, different areas of your business or project may benefit from activity on different social networking sites. For example, we have mentioned above that LinkedIn has become a favourite for professionals seeking new positions, so HR departments may find this more beneficial than activity on Facebook. A support department might get great interaction on Twitter because it's so quick and easy to ask questions and get a response.

If you have decided to share the responsibility of updating these social media sites with your colleagues or employees, make sure they understand what they are and are not allowed to post. Ensure that they feel able to respond to queries or know how to handle them if not. Don't delegate the task to someone who doesn't understand the boundaries of their new role.

Some larger companies include the dos and don'ts for social media activity in employee handbooks, contracts or guidelines. It's worth considering what your staff might be saying on their personal social media accounts about your project or people you might be working with. If you are allowing them to update the professional social media accounts, will they be tempted to sneak on to their own personal accounts? Don't hesitate to produce some guidelines to hand out to your staff if you are worried and discuss these with them further if they have queries.

Try it now: Assess a competitor's social media participation

Take a look at your competitor's websites again. What social media sites does it have profiles on? How many other people is it connected to on these sites? How often does it post or update its profiles? Does it have more than one account on each site? Make a few notes about its activity and how successful its attempts have been. What do you need to be doing that's the same as your competitor and what should you do differently?

Privacy

As with anything posted on the Internet, there are privacy issues surrounding all these social media sites. While there are terms of service in place, no one really ever reads them. As a general rule of thumb, it's always best not to put anything on the Web that might come back to haunt you later. Images, especially, can be a risky business because there is actually nothing stopping people saving images that you have posted to these sites. Yes, it's breaking terms of service but moral compasses don't always point true north and there's no way of knowing when your images are being used by someone else.

There's also the issue of people misusing information you post on your profiles. Facebook allows you to control who sees the updates you post but Twitter is much more public. As we are recommending that you get your project signed up to Twitter and/or Facebook, we will look at their privacy controls in more depth in the chapters devoted to them.

Remember this: Keep it private

Know what your privacy settings are – if you aren't happy with them, check the controls to see if they can be altered in any way. If the controls on offer don't create as tight a safeguard as you want, you just have to monitor what you post more strictly.

Posting

If you think back to Chapter 1, we hope you will remember the three things that anything you post online has to have:

1 **clarity** – so it's easy to read and understand

2 **purpose** – so there's a reason for someone to read it

3 **motivation** – so the reader is interested and wants to read more from you.

Posting updates on social media accounts that aren't of any use or interest to your target audience won't help you build a following. People won't connect with you if they aren't interested in what you have got to say. As you start out, think about your target audience each time you post and put yourself in their shoes. In time, posting this way will become a habit and you won't need to think about what you are posting. Review what you are about to post before actually hitting the button to send it and making it public.

Bear in mind, too, the writing etiquette we covered in Chapter 1: check your spelling and punctuation, don't ramble, and avoid slang and abbreviations!

Key idea: Four types of update

As a rule of thumb, there are only four different types of update:

1 **News** Letting your followers know when someone new joins your team, or when your project wins an award – it lets them feel valued

2 **Customer service** Reporting back on any issues that your clients or customers may be experiencing when working with your project

3 **Feedback** Publishing any new testimonials or comments reported back to you from clients or customers that reflect well on your project

4 **Special offers** Those interested in you can't know if you are running a promotion if you don't tell them about it!

Try it now: Mind-map™ ideas

Taking the four different types of update described above, make a note of any updates that you could post right now. Have you won any awards lately? Hired new staff? Been mentioned in the local news? Received a glowing testimonial? If there's anything that fits into the four types above, write it down. We will come back to this list in later chapters. If you can't think of anything, maybe because your project hasn't got fully underway yet, then don't worry – as your project grows, so will the number of things you can update people on.

REPLYING

It's important to reply to people who post to you on any social media site (spam excluded). It's an important step in humanizing your project – showing that someone is taking the time to read comments and feeding back to those connected on the sites. Even if you get negative feedback, it's better to reply than just ignore or delete the comment. Thinking it will go away won't get you anywhere – there could be a genuine issue with your project that does need your attention, so it's always a good idea to try to get to the bottom of the problem. Of course, if someone has left you positive feedback, always thank them!

You may even be able to use these comments as testimonials on your website, providing you get permission from the poster first.

Key idea: Respond positively to negative feedback

Never get into an online debate over a comment – ask those with negative feedback to email you privately.

Integrating: TweetDeck vs. HootSuite

As we have mentioned in some of the descriptions of the social networking sites above, they do allow cross-posting of content. You can link up your YouTube account to your Facebook and Twitter accounts so that, when you upload and publish a new video to YouTube, a link to that video will automatically get sent out on your Facebook and Twitter pages. These sites should always ask for permission to access these third-party sites first and will require you to log in to the site you want to access. These will be called applications – so, in the example given above, the YouTube application would request access to your Facebook and Twitter accounts.

If time isn't on your side, you need a program that makes it simple to update your profiles from one place at the same time. For us, there are two options that stand out – TweetDeck and HootSuite. When it comes to choosing the program for you, there are various factors to bear in mind.

COST

Knowing that most social networking sites are free to use, it can be a bit of a shock to be faced with having to pay for a third-party tool. If you are just starting out and finding your feet, you won't want to pay anything. TweetDeck is completely free and HootSuite offers two packages – free and pro. The pro package is $9.99 per month but you can take a 30-day trial to test it first before committing to paying anything.

The free versions on offer from both clients are pretty similar; differences only come into play when you start paying for the extra benefits. HootSuite Pro allows you to add unlimited social profiles to the accounts where the free version limits you to just five. It also integrates Google Analytics and Facebook Insights, which both help you work out just how effective your updates are.

INTERFACE

One of the differences between TweetDeck and HootSuite is that you can download TweetDeck to run from your desktop, whereas HootSuite is currently completely browser-based. TweetDeck also shows everything in one window, in different panels, which means you just have to scroll to the column you want to view.

HootSuite, on the other hand, contains your different profiles in different tabs and then different activities in those accounts displayed in columns, which can take a bit of figuring out. This also means that, if you are viewing the Facebook tab, you can't see what's happening on the Twitter tab, which – depending on your viewpoint – can be either good or bad. While it allows you to focus on one thing at a time, you could be missing out on something important elsewhere. By having the tabbed interface, HootSuite does make you pay more attention to the tab you are on, so you don't get accounts mixed up if you are posting from more than one organization. In TweetDeck the individual columns are headed by column type (e.g. Mentions, All Friends, Direct Messages) and then the name of that account, so you can become more easily confused than in HootSuite.

CROSS-NETWORK UPDATING

Which of the two programs to choose partly depends on just how many accounts you need to update. TweetDeck allows you to link only one Facebook account to it but you can then update the individual pages and groups under that account. HootSuite's free package allows you to add a total of five social profiles – this means you can have one Facebook profile, one page, one group and two Twitter accounts added before you will need to upgrade if you want to add a LinkedIn account. If you are just starting out, then you aren't likely to need more than five, so either provider will be suitable. However, the social media accounts they allow you to connect with do vary, so it's worth checking the list below in case one doesn't cater for the site you are using:

TweetDeck	HootSuite
Twitter	Twitter
Facebook	Facebook
LinkedIn	Google+
foursquare	LinkedIn
MySpace	foursquare
Buzz	MySpace
	WordPress
	mixi

Always bear in mind which accounts are set up to post to others, and in which direction they post. For example, you may have set your Twitter to post automatically to your Facebook account. This won't mean that Facebook will automatically post to Twitter. While this type of cross-posting can be beneficial (in the sense that your followers on one account will see that the update has come from another account and they can connect with you on there also), it can become a bit of a nightmare. If you had posted to Facebook first, you have also got to post to Twitter, which then means the update is going on Facebook again. Third-party updaters can be handy here, as you can post to both Twitter and Facebook at the same time with the same update, so you wouldn't need to have the Twitter application approved on your Facebook account, or vice versa.

Remember this: Posting

You do need to keep an eye on which accounts you are posting to. As we have mentioned, you can have more than one Facebook account set up for you to post to, and more than one Twitter. Always check which ones you have selected to post to and that the post is definitely relevant to that account — a vital thing to check if you are responsible for updating the accounts for more than one project.

Case study: Bright Yellow Marketing (www.brightyellowmarketing.com)

Sara Greenfield and her husband, Chris had owned their 'thebestof' franchise for many years, running the Norwich branch at full capacity, when they realized they could diversify their activities.

They had been turning several prospective clients away from thebestofNorwich for various reasons – these were local businesses which were looking for marketing advice. Bright Yellow Marketing was born as an alternative for these prospective clients, in order to offer them social media help and training.

While thebestofNorwich still provides social media services for its members, Bright Yellow Marketing is also at hand, running workshops and staff training days for those thebestofNorwich can't take on as members. The couple take clients right from the very basics of setting up a profile to analysing the impact of social media activities. Their advanced workshop – 'Social Media Monitoring' – came about at the request of local PR agencies.

Sara has worked with social media from the very beginning and admits that sites are very different now from what they used to be:

'Twitter was very effective in the early stages because there were fewer people on there, so it was easier to get to know people. Now there are a lot of people and a lot of other messages for you to be heard over. But, on the plus side, there are more tools available to ensure that your message gets to the right audience.

'We still find Twitter and LinkedIn highly effective for our clients' needs. The various platforms also provide a free, easy way to communicate with our own clients as well as promoting their businesses. Facebook has been great from a franchisee perspective because we have a Facebook group where we can share top tips and documents with other franchisees.'

SCHEDULING

If you are updating your accounts using one of the programs above, TweetDeck or HootSuite, you have the ability to 'queue' updates. This means you can type out the update you want to post, but instead of posting it as and when you write it, you can set a date and time for it to be sent in the future. This can be really handy if you haven't got time to update your accounts every day. You can simply queue a couple of updates to be posted each day.

Promoting

As we have mentioned, a lot of advertising now includes social media information. Any form of advert, whether it be print or digital, will contain a reference to a Facebook page or Twitter account. They are sneaking their way on to business cards, and links to social networking profiles are more often than not included in email signatures. Because so many people use various different networking sites, it's the easiest way to connect with your audience. So much potential is lost if you are not putting yourself out there in front of your audience. It also provides another super easy way for a potential or current client/customer to get in touch with you, both publicly and privately, and vice versa.

On social media

Robert says...

There are no longer any secrets in the world. Social media sees to that. Unfaithful footballers may gag print and broadcast media with injunctions, but the chambermaid can take a snap of the rumpled bed with her phone and post it on Facebook or tweet while he and his lover are still having breakfast. World events are increasingly reported on Twitter first, by people who are there, witnessing events that others retweet and share.

When I attend an event, I always make sure to get Wi-Fi access and tweet. Even if not invited to speak, I can influence people in the room online. Moreover, I can influence people outside the room, too, and that is often more important.

And social media allow you to engage people you would normally never speak with in dialogue. If I want to talk to national journalists, politicians or other thought leaders, I do it via Twitter.

Social media also eliminate national boundaries. My books are read worldwide and have helped me build a global network. It's not unusual to have a Facebook chat, in real time, with a budding entrepreneur sitting in an Internet café in rural West Africa.

Of course, there's a downside. Prince Harry discovered that when cavorting naked at a party. Images of his escapade were captured and shared within minutes by an indiscreet guest. For some, social media present an opportunity, while for others they are a threat!

Jess says...

As with my online messaging, when using social media for business purposes I have to maintain a professional image at all times in a way that focuses solely on promoting Robert's services, client news and projects.

I have access to Robert's social media accounts, which allows me to post out links to new media coverage and articles that either feature Robert or are written by him to encourage his followers to click through. His social media accounts are also linked to and from his website and can be reached from any page of his website. Whereas it used to be the case that those interested in Robert would have to visit his website for new content, the content now gets streamed directly in front of them via social media.

I use TweetDeck for posting new content – it's so easy to create the updates for both Facebook and Twitter and post instantly. Queuing posts can be a blessing, too, because it means I can still promote Robert on social media even when I'm on holiday!

Focus points

* Social networks allow you to connect online with like-minded people, but in order to keep the conversation and discussion going, you have to put in some effort.
* Remember that you are posting on behalf of your business, so post only necessary updates – maintain a professional image.
* Keep a friendly, approachable tone when posting and replying to people, even negative people!
* There are four types of update: news, customer service updates, feedback or special offers.
* Follow the writing etiquette rules we covered in Chapter 1!

Summary

So, now you know more about social networking and are able to list the names of the main social media sites. We have talked in general about posting updates to these sites and replying to those who respond. You should now know how third-party programs, TweetDeck and Hootsuite, work and how they can help and hinder you in trying to improve your online communication. In the next few chapters we will take an in-depth look at the biggest names – Facebook, Twitter and LinkedIn – and how you can get set up on them and posting.

Next step

In the next chapter we are taking a better look at Facebook. We are going to look at how the different pages that the site offers vary (profile, page and group) and how to fill in each section for the right page for your project.

Facebook

In this chapter you will learn:

▶ *about the terminology especially associated with Facebook, the world's number-one social media platform*

▶ *the difference between a profile, a Page and a group*

▶ *how to set up on Facebook quickly and easily*

▶ *about the options for advertising through Facebook.*

Self-assessment: What should I be using Facebook for?

Take the diagnostic test below as you have in the previous chapters and we will find out just what you need to be doing on this social media site.

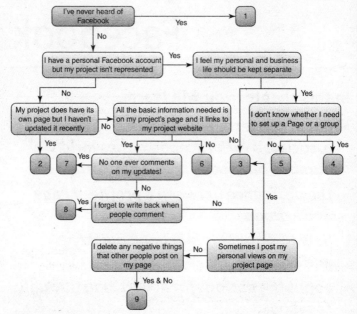

Feedback

1 You are part of the minority! It's very rare for someone to not have heard of Facebook, but don't worry – it's really easy to get the hang of once you get stuck in. We will give a brief overview of its background and walk you through getting a page or a group set up to represent your project.

2 If you have already got a following built up, you will still find much that is valuable in the following pages. We will be looking at what kind of content and updates you need to be posting to keep your page running smoothly.

3 This can be quite risky. If you ever need to give a personal opinion, it's best to distance yourself from the project and post under your own name. Your project clients won't be interested in what you get up to on a Friday night.

4   We will be going over the differences between a Page and a group to help you decide which is the best version to set up for your project.

5   Further on in this chapter we will cover how to write the different sections of your Page or group, so you will be able to get on and get started. Also check out the section on what material you should be posting.

6   All the sections you need to fill in for your Page or group are covered further on in this chapter.

7   You are probably not posting the right kind of updates or you are targeting the wrong audience. Remember, we looked at who you should be targeting in Chapter 2; you need to be writing for these people in an easy-to-understand way that will interest them. In this chapter we will look at the main different types of updates you can post on your Facebook Page or group.

8   You may not have the time to do this, but is there someone who could handle it for you? Don't be afraid to delegate the task, as it's important to keep discussions running on your page to keep members or fans returning.

9   Try to resolve any issues publicly to show others that you are willing to take on board any negative feedback. Ask the critic to get in touch by email so you can look into the matter further if the situation threatens to get out of hand. Thank people for feedback regardless of whether it is positive or negative.

An open place

'I'm trying to make the world a more open place.'
Mark Zuckerberg, Facebook co-founder

Facebook has become something you can't really escape from. It gets mentioned on the news, it tells you the latest gossip and, more importantly, it can get your news in front of your family, friends and clients immediately.

In fact, the challenge is not to be on Facebook but to differentiate between your social and professional networks. And, as with the rest of the Internet, it has its dark side. While most people keep to the terms of use, there are some who choose to cause plenty of trouble to others.

Almost half of the UK's population are registered Facebook users. The chances are there's an untapped audience waiting for you to target. Indeed, it's likely that you are already a confident Facebook user. But it is also likely that you have yet to fully exploit the professional or business potential that the network can provide.

You will be pleased to know that it's relatively simple to set up a professional, project or business group or page on Facebook. As with so much online promotion, the difficulty is finding the time, text and focus.

That's what we will be covering together in this chapter.

Facebook and other social media sites will also help boost your writing confidence online. This is because they are so immediate: once you know what your message and purpose are, you can post updates without really needing to think about them – although, of course, thinking about them is actually rather important.

Terminology

The following box contains a list of the terms frequently used with Facebook:

Apps Short for 'applications'. These can be quizzes, games and other social networking add-ons. If you add these to your page, every time you use the app an update will appear for others to see that you have used that app. For example, the *Guardian* has a Facebook app and, if you allow it access to your profile, it will automatically post an update every time you read an article on the *Guardian* 's app. (If you are aged over 45 it helps to think of apps as pieces of software.)

Block If you receive abuse from a person then you can block this person and they won't be able to contact you. You can also report this abuse and, in extreme cases, a user may have their account deleted from Facebook. You can also choose to block certain posts from appearing in your feed – for example, if you have liked a Page but they keep posting pictures from a specific application, then you can choose to block updates from that application. Then they will no longer appear in your feed.

Comments The feature that allows other people to add a remark either to an update you have posted or directly to your page.

Fans The people who have liked a page.

Feed This is basically a homepage tailored to each and every Facebook user. It's a long streaming list of all the updates that any user's friends, liked Pages or joined groups have posted, in reverse chronological order.

Likes There are two different types of likes but they are both actions to show a user likes something. You can 'like' a Page – this will mean that you will get that Page's content streamed straight to your feed and that you can be contacted by the administrators of that Page along with the other users who have liked that Page. You can also 'like' content – if a friend, group or Page uploads or posts something that you like, you can show them by clicking the little thumbs-up icon that will appear underneath the update.

Members The people who have joined a group.

Post/update/status The content that people publish on Facebook that will appear on pages.

Profile/group/Page The three different types of page you can have within Facebook. Users befriend profiles, join groups and like Pages. Profiles are intended for personal purposes rather than commercial ones – every person who signs up to get a Facebook account starts off with a profile which they fill out with information about them as a person. Then they can add additional Pages and groups. We will go into Pages and groups in a bit more detail later in the chapter.

Timeline This is a relatively new term for a new style profile that has recently been introduced. The content that gets posted to a profile, Page or group is their timeline. It's basically a reverse chronological listing of the things they have posted. A dated line will appear down the middle of the page with updates posted to the left and right of this line.

Wall The space on your profile where you and others who are connected to you can post.

Background

Forty-nine per cent of the UK population are signed up to Facebook. You can reach any part of that audience: by contacting friends of friends; by searching and then messaging, or by placing Facebook ads that can allow you to target an audience very accurately. Whatever you are trying to do, sell or achieve, Facebook can help. There's even a movie about it – *The Social Network* (2010).

As with the Internet in general, Facebook started off as a way for people to get in touch. Rather than being a forum that allowed scientists to share data, Facebook's purpose was social. Originally launched to allow alumni students to keep in touch, it quickly grew in popularity and soon spread beyond university campuses.

Today Facebook is widely used by people of all ages. In fact, older people, for whom isolation and loneliness can be the real problems, find that Facebook gives them 'on demand' social interaction with a wide and eclectic range of people.

Why use Facebook?

Facebook is a powerful marketing tool for those who recognize its potential to gain access to otherwise hard-to-reach or expensive-to-reach demographic groups. The sheer size of Facebook makes it perfect for sharing. If your project has a lot of news and content to share, and you have got an audience to tell, then Facebook is the easiest place from which to do so. Facebook also makes it really easy to add videos and photos to share.

SOME STATISTICS TO BEAR IN MIND

In May 2012 it was reported that in the UK:

▷ the number of users had reached 30,945,100 (and this number grows daily)

▷ the majority of these users are female (52 per cent)

▷ the largest age group represented among the UK users was the 25–34s

▷ Facebook gets an average of more than 1.3 billion UK visits a month

▷ on average, each Facebook fan brings an additional 20 visits to your website over the course of a year

▷ Facebook was the second most visited site after Google and follows it as the second largest referrer of all website traffic.

Key idea: It's where your audience is

No matter how niche a market your project serves, or rarefied the industry you work in, it's virtually guaranteed that there will be an audience for you on Facebook. As with any online marketing, it's worth putting in the time and effort to keep your Facebook account up to date with your latest news and content. If you start off on the right track, build yourself up a good audience of followers, and then stop your efforts, you won't have gained anything. Sure, you can always build the audience back up, but you will have lost that initial momentum. What's important is to set a manageable pace and then maintain it.

AVOID...

▷ **...assuming it's just for teenagers** – adults of all ages like to share things, too! The user appeal about Facebook is its universality. You can find almost anybody, interested in almost anything, through its search facility. For example, people who were adopted as babies have found birth family members through Facebook.

▷ **...setting yourself up with a Page or group for your project, encourage people to join it and then ignore it.** People will forget the page is there and won't be inclined to comment if you don't share. Get into the habit of posting content regularly and inviting feedback from those who have liked your Page. (In fact, if you feel able, it is better to *provoke* feedback than simply invite it.) If someone asks a question, answer it! If someone comments on how good something was, reply!

Also bear in mind that Facebook is first and foremost for social use, not business. If you do the 'hard sell' on people here, they will be put off. You need to learn to keep the equilibrium between pushing your project and keeping things light-hearted and welcoming.

Remember this: Get involved!

Facebook is all about sharing with like-minded people – don't forget that conversations have to involve two or more people. You have to get involved, too. Facebook should be for life and not just Christmas!

Signing up

Getting on to Facebook is easy, even if you don't have an account already. You will need to have an account in order to set up a Page or a group for your project. To set up a group or a Page, you need to register yourself and have a profile. Officially, profiles aren't meant for commercial use under Facebook's terms of use.

Remember that you do not have to post personal information on a Facebook profile that you create. You are in control of the page and can edit content that others who know you may add. In other words, your personal Facebook profile will only be as personal as you choose to make it.

Let's assume that your focus is to create a professional Page or group. Your profile page simply becomes the place from which you manage your user account.

There's an 'administrators' feature which makes it easier to update content. This in particular means that other members of your team or staff can update the Page or group. Then you can share the work between you.

By creating a Page or group under a personal account, you have the opportunity to add personal comments to what is a professional or project Page or group. This enables you to develop your own online personality, adding your own perspectives to the project Page or group.

So, sign yourself up to Facebook to create an account for yourself. Then, from there, create a Page or group for your project. Pages should only be set up by an official representative of the organization, business, band or celebrity that the Page is to promote.

It should be noted that a user cannot have duplicate accounts – if you want to set yourself up with a work profile and a personal profile, then think again. Facebook may delete one account without warning.

Remember this: Page vs. group

	Page	Group
Privacy	Content is public and mostly available to anyone with a Facebook account.	Three options: Open – anyone on Facebook can view content and become a member Closed –members must be invited or approved before having access to content Secret – can't be found in searches so non-members have minimum access to the page. A member must be added by an administrator or member.
Audience	Anybody with a Facebook account can 'like' the Page to receive new updates streamed straight to their feed. There is no limit to how many fans a Page can have.	Members can be approved or invited by an administrator/ member of the group. The smaller the audience, the more features the group has access to.
Communication	Administrators can share content under the Page name or choose to post on behalf of themselves.	Members receive notifications by default if a friend of theirs posts on that group. Members can upload photos and invite friends to join the group also.

Your profile

You may not use your profile much for promoting your project; it may be purely a Page or group you promote. However, if your project is very much based on you – for example, if you are doing some form of freelance work – then it is worth taking the time to fill your profile out with as much information as possible as you may personally be connecting with some of your clients. Your profile needs:

▶ **your correct name** – so people can easily find you

▶ **a profile picture** – so people can recognize you (handy if you have got a common name)

▶ **basic information** – so people can learn more about you (note that you can choose the extent to which personal information is visible or hidden on your profile page)

▶ **a link to your website** – so people can find out more about what you do

▶ **contact details** – your phone number and email address.

Finally, you will see that you can send and receive private messages between Facebook users. This can be useful when you want to approach somebody new. It also enables you to 'chat' with other people online at the same time as you.

Key idea: Privacy

You will remember that when people 'like' your Page, content you add will appear automatically on their Facebook feed. Anything that you post here will be visible to anyone who chooses to look for it. This means that your posts are not exclusive or purely visible to just your audience. Remember that rivals and competitors will also be looking at your Page.

With a group, settings can be put in place so that Facebook users have to request to join or be added by other members. In the event of requesting to join a group, the administrators of the group will get an email saying a certain user has requested to join the group and they can either accept or decline.

While anyone can view a Page, you can restrict access to your group. So you could have a personal profile when you connect with your professional network, a product or project Page visible to all, and an exclusive group for the select inner circle.

Individual profiles have different privacy settings that you can change. You have three different options when it comes to the visibility of this page:

1 You can make your whole profile public to anyone else on Facebook.

2 Your 'activity' (for example, any recent friends you have added, but not updates) can be viewable by anyone.

3 Only friends can see your profile.

You can check and change your privacy settings at any time, so, if you find that one setting doesn't work out for you, you can easily change it.

For example:

> James works for a major telecoms provider. His job involves supporting a group of product users, each of whom is a subscriber to his company's specialist broadband service. He is also a product specialist providing technical support and information about his specific area of expertise.

He decides to use Facebook as a convenient way to communicate with his clients. He's already Facebook friends with half a dozen of those he knows best and suspects that almost all his clients have a Facebook account.

After tidying up his personal profile, James creates a Facebook Page where he posts technical information. He also links this Page with his Twitter account so that software tips and fixes to glitches and encounters are instantly fed to his Page the moment he tweets them. He is happy for competitors to see this information as well as their own clients.

Finally he sets up a group. He invites users to join the group through his existing network of Facebook friends. Others who hear of the group also ask to join. James allows in only those with current maintenance contracts. He then uses the group to stimulate and support dialogue between users. This is valuable both to those users and also for giving him market feedback that enables him to understand how the product is used and what additional features might be useful.

He could have done all of it with a bespoke product website connected to his company's website. But by using Facebook, an application he knows most of his clients have open on their PC throughout the working day, he has created a far more dynamic, interactive and, most importantly, well-used resource. And it has cost absolutely nothing apart from the time it took to set up.

Creating a Page or group

Whether you choose to set up a Page or a group, it's worth remembering that you will be able to contact anyone who connects with that Page. If you get 50 people to like a Page (fans) or to join a group (members), you can send a message to those 50 people all at the same time.

YOUR NAME

This will usually be your project name, just to make it as easy as possible for people to find you in search results. If you ever change your group or Page name, make sure you have posted this out as news well in advance to let your fans or followers know, otherwise they won't know who you are when they see posts under your new name in their feed. Try to keep the name as short and as specific as possible to keep it user-friendly.

SECTIONS OF A PAGE

Before you even start writing anything for your Page, you need to make sure you have got the most appropriate option selected for the Page's category. There are 11 different categories to choose from:

- Books & Magazines
- Brands & Products
- Companies & Organizations
- Local Business
- Movies
- Music
- Other
- People
- Sports
- Television
- Websites & Blogs

There are then even further subcategories to choose from. Choose the one that best matches your project, as these categories and subcategories are useful in that they drive the way Facebook's search function operates.

It's important to make sure you have got the right category selected, as each type has different sections to fill in. For example, selecting the Local Business category will let you enter your opening hours and whether you have parking facilities or not; this is hardly applicable if you are trying to promote a single product or an individual. The Books & Magazines category with Books subcategory will let you enter a publisher and ISBN number, and if you choose the Actor/Director subcategory under the Movies category, you could add a Biography section. We will walk you through the most common sections that appear on the majority of, but not all, Page categories available. You don't have to fill in each section but the more information you can put on your Page, the better.

▶ Official Page

This section allows you to link to another Page if you are not an official representative of what your Page is about. For example, your Page could be about a brand – if you don't actually represent that brand, you should enter the name of that official Page in this section. Obviously, if you are representing the organization, brand, person (or other) that your Page is about, you don't have to fill this section in.

▶ Username

This is basically the unique URL of your Facebook page. This allows you to direct people straight to this URL rather than provide instructions about how to search for your page. Every username will start with the Facebook URL (www.facebook. com); then you add on: /YourUsername. Make it something easy to remember and definitely keep it relevant to your page. Facebook guidelines say that the username must be as close to the name of your page as possible. You can also only use alphanumeric characters (0–9, a–z) or periods (.) and a username should consist of at least one letter. Although you can have only one username per Page, you are able to change the username when you like, so you are not fixed to the same one for ever (handy if you make a spelling mistake...). This means you can get the URL printed on business cards and other advertising, or even include it in your email signature.

▶ Name

This is the name of your Page – it will show up in Facebook searches and at the top of your Page when someone visits it. This should be as close to your project name as possible. For example, if you were running ABC Gardening then ABC Gardening should be your Facebook Page name.

▶ Start date

This is when your Page's timeline will begin. Remember that the timeline is the presentation of any posts and updates on your Page. This means that if you set a Page up a while back but haven't updated it, you can set the start date to a more recent point. This also means that any content that was posted before the start date will no longer appear – giving your Page a completely fresh start. You can enter the year, month and even a day if you want a really specific cut-off point. If you are starting a new Page from scratch, simply make this section the date you are starting the Page. Mostly, though, it's a good idea to make this date the actual date your project started because this start date will be displayed next to the option below...

▶ Start type

There are six different options displayed here on a drop-down menu:

- ▶ Born

- ▶ Founded

- ▶ Started

- ▶ Opened

- ▶ Created

- ▶ Launched

You basically pick the one that is most relevant to your project. If your page represents a shop, you would probably choose 'Opened'; if it is an organization you might choose 'Launched' or 'Founded'.

▶ Address

Let people know where you are based – it can help them determine if you are the right project they are looking for if there are several pages with similar names. You can use either your physical location or your registered address. If you receive visitors, put your actual location. Some projects don't have an office and so use an accountant or similar as their registered address.

▶ About

This section needs to summarize what it is you do and who you are. This information will be displayed on your Page under your profile picture and Page title. It's usually kept to about one or two sentences. There is a 255-character limit (including spaces) on this section, so you are limited to what you can say. Make sure this section includes the most vital information anyone visiting your Page would need to know. If you are pushed for what to write, take a look at your website – it should already contain all the information you need for this section and the following two sections described below. You may just be able to copy and paste. Include any keywords you can fit in – and include them in the description and mission, where possible.

▶ Description

Here's where you can add a little more detail about your project. Cover everything you do and include a bit of history about the project if you have been going for a while; or let people know if you have just started up. Mention any awards you have won or any accreditations. Make sure to include a link to your website here, too – you don't need to worry about adding the http:// prefix; Facebook will convert the Web address to a hyperlink automatically.

▶ Mission

Reiterate why you are doing what you are doing – what are the goals of your project? Have you got any deadlines you need to meet? Is there something you need your audience to do to help you achieve your targets? Put any calls to action here.

▶ Phone number

This number will be visible to those who visit your Page or who 'like' it (depending on your privacy settings), so make sure it's the right one!

▶ Email

As with the telephone number, ensure that there are no errors when you type this out, as this will prevent people contacting you.

SECTIONS OF A GROUP

There are fewer options available when it comes to editing a group. You don't have the option to select a category for your group. You simply have the following sections:

▶ Group name

As with the Page name, this is the heading that the group will have and will appear in search results and at the top of the page.

▶ Privacy

We touched on this briefly earlier in the chapter. Here there are three different selections you can choose from:

1 **Open** – anyone can see the group, who's in it and what members post

2 **Closed** – anyone can see the group and who's in it, but only members can see posts

3 **Secret** – only members can see the group, who's in it and what members have posted.

Remember that secret groups can't be found in search results, so the only way someone can find you is if they are invited to join that group. By choosing this option you would be stopping people from just stumbling on your page – which could be a good or bad thing but really does depend on your aims for being on Facebook. Open groups are completely visible to anyone on Facebook, which means that anyone can comment, whereas with closed groups Facebook users have to be a member of your group to comment on something you have posted.

Key idea: The opted-in mailing list

All members of a Facebook group can be contacted simultaneously – by joining your group, a user has agreed that they don't mind you contacting them (so long as you don't abuse that privilege by sending them spam). If you are just starting out and want to begin building a list of those who are interested in you, it's best to start out with a closed group to ensure that people who join the group do so to get the most out of the group discussions. You therefore know that they want to know more about you and you can contact them at a later stage via a Facebook message.

▶ Membership approval

As with the privacy section above, you have a choice to make here:

▶ *either:* any member can add or approve members

▶ *or:* any member can add members, but an administrator must approve them.

This is basically giving you the option to approve who joins your group and has access to the content. If you choose to approve people, make sure they aren't left waiting – approve or decline their membership in a reasonable space of time.

▶ Group address

This is where you set up the unique URL for your group. It has an additional benefit, however. Clicking the 'Set up Group Address' button will bring up a screen that allows you to set an email address for your group. This means that, when you send an email to this address (yourgroupaddress@groups.facebook. com), all the members in your group will receive that email as a Facebook message. Whatever you set the yourgroupaddress section to will also become your group's URL (www.facebook. com/groups/yourgroupaddress). You want to make sure that you keep this as short and as memorable as possible, while still keeping it close to whatever you have called your group.

▶ Description

This details what your group is about. This section is viewable by anyone visiting an open or closed group, but not a secret group. Here you should be concise and use as many keywords as possible, as keyword searches will match with anything you have written in this box. Also make sure to include any specific contact details that might be useful for your members to have – a telephone number, email address, website, etc. – as you won't have an option to include these separately.

▶ Posting permissions

This section controls who can post on the group's feed – only members or only administrators.

Advertising

Facebook offers small advertising spaces – these are the small blocks displayed along any Facebook page to the right, which display Facebook Ads or Sponsored Stories. As with most advertising, it costs you to appear here, but you can set yourself budgets to ensure that you aren't spending more than you can afford.

FACEBOOK ADS

When setting your ad up, you are able to choose not only keywords and demographics (such as age, gender, location) but also the job titles of those who might be most interested in your project. This all helps narrow down the number of Facebook users to those who will find your adverts interesting. This ensures that your ads are shown only to a relevant audience, ultimately making the most of your money if the ad has been done well.

You then choose how you want to pay for your adverts – do you want to pay for each click you get or each view? Generally, people go for 'pay per click' instead of 'pay per view' (or, as Facebook calls it, 'cost per impression'), as that way you only pay for those who are actually visiting the page you are promoting. Set yourself a budget you can manage and Facebook won't go over this limit.

Initially, try experimenting with the text you use in your advert. Play with the words you want to use to find which format brings the best results. As a rule of thumb, it's always best to include:

▶ a clear call to action in the body text to get your audience to do something

▶ any benefits or special offers that your project is offering

▶ a clear, eye-catching image relative to your project and text

▶ a project name, so anyone clicking through will know they have arrived on an appropriate page.

For example:

> Amelia is a fundraiser for her local hospice. She has successfully grown her organization's Facebook presence and now has several hundred people who like her page. She also has a closed donor group. Here, her regular supporters discuss fundraising ideas among themselves. She finds this immensely useful.
>
> Now Amelia is organizing a summer ball. She wants to use it to attract new potential donors to a network. She knows, from the existing audience, the kind of people they will be, in terms of age, location and interests. She creates an ad to sell corporate tables at her summer ball.
>
> Amelia sets herself a budget of £50 and carefully targets her Facebook ad so that it is only going to be seen by the people most like her existing supporters. As each corporate table she sells will raise £500, she is confident that even a couple of enquiries will make that £50 money well spent. As it happens, she sells three tables to people who contact her through the ad.

SPONSORED STORIES

These are adverts that promote a connection a Facebook user has made with your Page or group. These adverts are then displayed to that user's friends. These friends recognize that that person has interacted with you and will be encouraged to interact as well. It's a way of showing that your fans or members have endorsed your content. Sponsored stories ensure that this connection isn't lost among other updates in news feeds, prominently displaying the connection to the right-hand side of a Facebook page.

Case study: English Cheesecake Company (www.englishcheesecake.com)

Before proceeding with Facebook advertising, the English Cheesecake Company thought about exactly what it wanted to see happen as a result of its ad campaign. Importantly, it set some goals. It wanted to at least double its current amount of fans, widening its audience and giving it the opportunity to involve its fans in the development of new products. The company also wanted to increase the number of repeat purchases and increase customer spend, knowing that it could do this by boosting its fan engagement.

There were two streams to its campaign: ads and Page interaction. The adverts would draw more people to the Page, and the Page interaction would draw more people into feeding back on suggested new products, and eventually buy.

The English Cheesecake Company used its page for different activities:
* Through polls, fans were able to vote for their favourite cheesecakes and the top ten became the Christmas product range.
* A dedicated member of staff was tasked with the job of answering all customer service questions.
* A competition was run to name the Royal Wedding Cheesecake, back in April 2011 (Willi-Yum and Cheese-Kate were the winners).
* After getting fan requests, they made the decision to launch a gluten-free range.

Through Facebook ads and sponsored stories, the organization was able to target those with similar interests, such as 'cheesecake' and 'bakery', and also their core target audience of UK-based females aged between 25 and 35.

As a result of their campaign, the English Cheesecake Company's Facebook fan base grew over 11 times in one year, taking their fans from 2,000 to 23,000 (more than 4,500 of whom came from sponsored stories alone). They found that 30 per cent of their new customers were coming to them from Facebook.

Posting updates and sending messages

Updates are the quickest and easiest way of getting something new out to your friends, fans or members, but not the most direct. Although you can post an update so it will be visible on your page, there's no guarantee that every friend, fan or member will see it.

Yes, the update will appear in their feed but they have to be online at the precise moment you publish the update to see it, visit your page specifically, or scroll back through past updates on their feed to see yours, which many people do. Private, direct messages can be sent to individual people connected to your page or as a mass message to everyone connected.

Remember this: Types of update

We covered this in the previous chapter but it's useful to recap here. If your update doesn't fall into any of the four main categories of update, you really should be thinking hard about whether you need to post it or not. The four different kinds of update are: news, customer service, feedback and special offers.

Keep anything personal away from your project pages. If you ever do post anything by mistake, you can quickly delete it, but in some cases – for example, if you are replying to a comment – the other people in the conversation will get an email with your comment in it. It's best to avoid making the mistake in the first place!

Try it now : Your first post!

You may not have any members or fans, but that's OK. Just head to your Page or group and click in the box where it says 'Write something'. Type something generic about you joining Facebook, such as, 'We have finally joined Facebook! For more information on what we do, visit our website www.yourwebsiteaddress.co.uk or call Bob on 01234 567 890.' Or pull out that mind map™ of ideas you made back in Chapter 4 and write about one of these.

On Facebook

Robert says...

Facebook suffers from a crisis of identity. What started out as an aid to on-campus networking has become a global social network. Boundaries between business and private life become blurred. Prospective employers may pay more attention to your Facebook profile than references from previous employers. It can be very confusing.

To me, Facebook is a place to reveal more of my personal life to those who might find it interesting. It's also a forum where I can chat with people I work with, in a non-work environment. I am Facebook friends with a number of influential people and our exchanges here are quite different from what we 'discuss' anywhere else.

Facebook can be the online equivalent of going for a drink with someone, or meeting them with their kids. You connect on a deeper, more personal level and that can help work relationships develop and grow.

To go further, I will deliberately choose the medium I use to communicate to match the message and the level. For example, I'll email someone about a proposal I want them to consider and perhaps share at work. I'll Facebook message them about the more emotional, feeling-based aspects of that same project.

Facebook is an inner layer of the onion of human interaction, next to the core of face-to-face contact, and deeper than Twitter or email.

Jess says...

Facebook is mainly used at work to promote new content by, or featuring, Robert. I also set up events pages and invite my connections to these events. They can then let me know if they are attending or not at the simple click of a button.

Separating business and personal activity on Facebook can be an issue. I had a Facebook profile before I started in full-time employment, so I was obviously used to the personal side of it and have had to integrate safeguards to ensure that my personal activity isn't seen by anyone with whom I have a business relationship.

My updates are quite different from Robert's! Creating lists of friends allows me to pick and choose which lists have access to different updates on my profile. All my updates are viewable only by friends and people not connected to me can't see what I'm posting.

Focus points

✳ Post only necessary updates to your Facebook Page or group, not pointless or irrelevant information – remember that you are posting on behalf of your project.

✳ Keep a friendly and approachable tone when replying to comments; avoid starting an argument with a fan or member. If there's really a problem, ask them to email you a private message.

✳ Avoid slang and abbreviations – be professional at all times.

✳ Post either news, customer service updates, feedback or special offers, and get involved in discussions on your page.

✳ Don't mix up your personal profile and your business page when posting updates – there are some things you won't want your clients or customers to know!

Summary

Congratulations! You should now have a Facebook page or group and be ready to let your current audience know that you have got it. If you already have a mailing list set up, include a link to the Page or group each time you distribute news, encouraging people to 'like' or 'join' it. Edit your email signature so this includes a direct link, too – then anyone you email will know where to find you on Facebook. Tell friends and family, too; they are always a good source of support and they can promote your page for free!

→ Next step

We have now got you set up on Facebook, so the next social network to tackle is Twitter. It's a lot more straightforward than Facebook as there's only the one kind of page you can post from – for now, anyway...

Twitter

In this chapter you will learn:

- *the terminology associated with Twitter*
- *how to sign up to a Twitter account*
- *how to attract a target following*
- *how to use hashtags effectively*
- *how to write the perfect 140-character tweet.*

Self-assessment: What should I be using Twitter for?

Take the diagnostic test below, as you have for the previous chapters, and we will find out just what you need to be doing on this social media site.

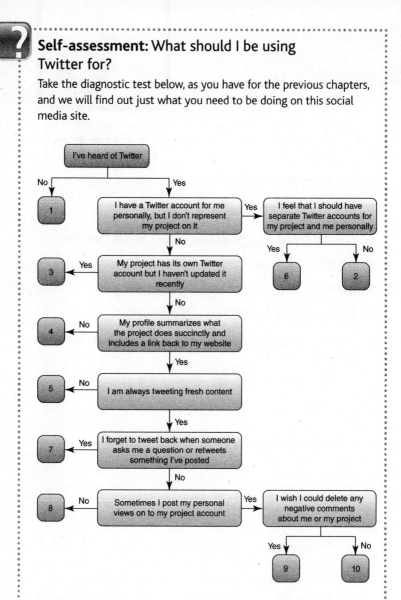

Feedback

1 It's a rare thing for someone not to have heard of Twitter, since hashtags are now invariably used for TV programmes and handles are being included on adverts. But don't worry – we will cover all aspects of Twitter in this chapter.

2 It's potentially dangerous to post both personal views and updates from your project under the one account. If you ever need to give a personal opinion, it's always best to distance yourself from the project to avoid any mix-up. Plus, the people you work alongside probably won't be interested in reading about what you got up to at the weekend.

3 If you have already got some people following you on Twitter, they are probably wondering where you have got to if you haven't posted anything or tweeted for a while. In this chapter we will be looking at the different things you can update your followers on. If time is something you are short of, then think about delegating the task.

4 Don't worry – we will be looking at how to fill out a Twitter profile and what you should be including.

5 Time may be an issue for you or perhaps you don't know what you should be tweeting about. We are going to look at how you can manage your time more effectively by delegating, and also what kinds of updates you should be posting to your Twitter account.

6 No problem – we agree. The only time it's OK not to separate the two is if you are the project. For example, Robert tweets using @RobertAshton1 and his followers hear about what he's up to because that's his business. If you are self-employed or on contract/freelance work, then who you are as a person will be of interest to those looking to work with you or hire you; not so much so if you need to represent a whole organization.

7 It's always good to remember to thank someone for a retweet as this will encourage them to do it again in the future. If you are finding it difficult to find the time to reply to those who tweet you, we have got a section in this chapter on how you can delegate the task or simply manage your time better so you can reply.

8 See number 6.

9 & 10 Welcome criticism with open arms and show your followers that you are willing to work on any issues. As with any other public feedback, though, don't challenge those who are negative and avoid inflaming the situation. If a situation looks as if it could get out of hand, simply ask the person to email you or message you privately to discuss the matter further. Always thank people for getting in touch.

Speed and intimacy

'...we came across the word "twitter", and it was just perfect. The definition was "a short burst of inconsequential information," and "chirps from birds." And that's exactly what the product was.'

Jack Dorsey, co-founder of Twitter

Although Twitter is not as old as Facebook, its user base is certainly expanding. It's become one of the quickest ways to build and communicate with an audience. It even describes itself as 'The fastest, simplest way to stay close to everything you care about.' It has more than 500 million worldwide users and has become one of the top 10 most visited websites.

In the UK, more people have a Twitter account than read a national daily newspaper. Stephen Fry, perhaps one of the best-known users, has 4.7 million followers. The appeal, perhaps, is its immediacy and – if tweets are written well – perceived intimacy between the followers and the followed. Stephen Fry, for example, tweets to give his followers an insight into his life and thoughts to a degree otherwise inaccessible to all but his closest friends.

The site is extremely similar to Facebook, in that it lets you share comment, photos, and videos with those who have connected with you and want to receive updates from you. The differences are that you are limited to a 140-character tweet for each of your updates and Twitter is much more public.

Although it doesn't feature as heavily in the news as Facebook, some of the hashtags that originate on Twitter have become news stories in their own right – the best known perhaps being *#riotcleanup*.

Terminology

Activity A real-time stream of what those you follow have been up to; whom they have just followed, what they just retweeted and which tweets they just favourited (see entry below).

Connect A list of tweets that mention you, or your tweets that have been retweeted and favourited. Also includes the latest Twitter accounts to start following you.

Direct message (DM) A private Tweet that can be seen only by the sender and the recipient.

Favourite Let people know you like their Tweet by clicking the little star next to it; this is favouriting.

FF/#FF Follow Friday – a hashtag that has become incredibly popular, to let followers know whom you recommend that they follow, too.

Follow This is the action that subscribes you to a user's tweets. A follower is someone who is subscribed to your tweets and will receive them in the stream on their home page.

Hashtag Using a # symbol in front of a keyword or topic turns it into a hashtag that can be followed. There must not be any spaces or punctuation between letters in a phrase as this will break up the link that the hashtag becomes.

Handle/username The account name that someone has chosen to go by when signing up for Twitter. It will appear in the URL of that user's profile. A username can be changed as often as the user likes.

Heard through/Hat tip (HT) A way of acknowledging a source of information used in a tweet. Someone may have originally posted a link that you want to repost but include your own text.

Home A real-time list of tweets from the Twitter users that you follow.

Lists Groups of Twitter users that have something in common. For example, you can start a 'Football players' list and add all the football players you follow to that list.

Mention When another Twitter user includes your username in a Tweet they have published.

Modified tweet (MT) Placed in front of a tweet that a user has modified from another Twitter user.

Profile A real-time list of a Twitter user's tweets. It also displays a short section on that user and, from here, lists of who follows them and who they follow can be accessed.

Promoted tweet Tweets that selected businesses have paid to promote at the top of search results on Twitter.

Retweet (RT) 1 (*verb*) To share a tweet from another user.

2 (*noun*) A tweet that has been shared.

Trending topic A subject that is determined to be one of the most talked-about topics on Twitter.

Tweet 1 (*verb*) To post an update on Twitter.

2 (*noun*) An update that has been posted on Twitter.

Tweet button A button that you can add to your website to allow visitors to post a link from that page straight to Twitter to share with their own followers.

Unfollow To unsubscribe from a user's tweets.

Verified account An account that Twitter acknowledges is the true account of a highly sought user in key interest areas or an individual at high risk of impersonation. Twitter adds a little white tick in a blue circle next to their username to distinguish them from non-verified users.

Background

Twitter was created back in March 2006 by Jack Dorsey and was launched in the July of that year. Originally, twttr (as it was first called) was intended to be a micro-blogging site that would be updated by text messages sent from mobile phones.

The popularity of Twitter is said to have taken off when screens displaying Twitter messages were shown at the South by Southwest Interactive Conference in 2007, which led to daily tweets increasing from 20,000 to 60,000. In that year there were 400,000 tweets being sent each quarter. This rose to 100 million tweets per quarter a year later. In February 2010, 50 million tweets were being sent per day.

On 21 March 2012, celebrating its sixth birthday, the site announced that it now had 140 million users, who collectively sent 340 million tweets each day. Because the site is very much focused on the immediacy of updates, it experiences usage spikes during prominent events. Michael Jackson's death caused the site servers to crash when updates were being sent at 100,000 tweets per hour. Twitter can still be updated by SMS from your phone, as well as through third-party applications, mobile apps, and online at twitter.com.

Why use Twitter?

Twitter is perfect for updating your followers on news as and when it happens. The character limit on updates means they have to be succinct and to the point, meaning they take less time to put together and the content can be out in the public domain quickly. Indeed, its succinct nature is what makes it so appealing to journalists. They use Twitter to find news and, more importantly for you, comment.

Key idea: It's where your audience is

Although Twitter can be seen to be more business-dominated than consumer-dominated, who's to say you can't spread your message to other businesses, too? Twitter has a wide user base and there are guaranteed to be other people who share your views – you have just got to put the time and effort into keeping your profile lively and appealing to these people.

Signing up

Getting yourself on Twitter is very straightforward. As with any other site you sign up to, you do need a valid email address in order to verify your identity and prove that you are a real person. This email address cannot already be associated with a different Twitter account, so if you get a notification to say that the email address is already in use, either get a password reminder issued so that you can sign in and edit that account, or simply (create and) use another email address.

Head over to www.twitter.com and fill in your full name, email address and password on the homepage and click 'Sign up for Twitter'. Remember to choose a password that's memorable to you but not obvious for other people to guess. You will then need to choose a username. If you are going to be representing a project, it's best to choose the name of the project but this name has to be less than 16 characters long and can't include the words 'Twitter' or 'Admin', to avoid any confusion.

Remember that this username is how people will find you and that it will also be included in the URL of your profile. You won't be able to have a username that someone else is using. You are able to change your username at any time, so, if you are not satisfied with the one you choose to begin with, don't worry. We don't recommend frequently changing your username, though, as it will confuse your followers – they will be expecting tweets from the username they followed, not someone else!

Your profile

Much more straightforward than Facebook, Twitter allows only one type of profile, so you don't need to worry about choosing the right type of page for your project's needs. There are fewer sections of the profile to fill out so it won't take you as long as it does to set up a Facebook account.

YOUR NAME

This is different from your username and can be your actual name, so that people know who's handling the tweets from your project. Alternatively, if you have had to scrimp on your username because there weren't enough characters available for you to fit in your whole project name, here's where you can put the full title. If you have used an obscure username, the name you use will help people track you down. The name can, of course, match the username, so you don't have to use your real name.

YOUR LOCATION
Let people know where you are. This is handy if there are other Twitter accounts with similar usernames, to prevent people following the wrong one. It also helps you track down businesses and other projects that are local to you.

YOUR WEBSITE
Always include a link back to your website. If a Twitter user finds your account and wants to discover more, they will use the link to visit your website and learn more about who you are and what it is that you do.

YOUR BIO
Twitter really likes character limits and here you have only 160 of them to summarize your project. You need to be really specific and clear – some bios (biographies) only contain single keywords, so no one is expecting you to use full sentences. Abbreviations are also acceptable as long as they are understandable. But don't use textspeak for the sake of it! Draft out your bio on a word processor with a built-in word counter and play around with the words until they fit within the 160-character limit.

Example:

Robert Ashton

@robertashton1

An outspoken, somewhat maverick social entrepreneur, business author and speaker; intelligent, insightful Robert holds nothing back and says it like he sees it!

FACEBOOK
This section gives you the option to synchronize your Twitter account with your Facebook account. This will allow Twitter to post your tweets direct to Facebook as and when you post them. We covered an alternative way of doing this through a

third-party application back in Chapter 4. If you do connect your two accounts in this way but decide at a later date that you want to stop the connection, simply come back to edit your profile and click 'Disconnect' in this section.

When editing your profile, always remember to click 'Save changes'; otherwise all your changes will be lost!

YOUR WEBSITE

You can use a Twitter widget to add your live Twitter stream to your website homepage. This both keeps your homepage up to date and shows that you are active and involved in your professional world.

Try it now: Sign up and fill in your profile!

Go online to www.twitter.com and follow the steps to sign up. Once you have picked a username that you are happy with, fill out the sections we have covered above. They are so easy to fill out that there's no reason to skip a bit. The hardest task will probably be summarizing what you do in 160 characters. Test out some ideas on a word processor to get the mix of words that works best and fits within the limit.

Following

On Facebook you 'friend', 'like' or 'join' a page to get its updates posted to your homepage; on Twitter you 'follow'. These are four different words for broadly the same function. There are three points to note about following:

1 A standard account can only follow up to 2,000 accounts. You will get a technical message pop up when you try to follow beyond your 2,000 limit. There is a relationship between your follower count and following count – a follow limit may be enforced sooner if you are following many people but have very few followers yourself. If there are other people you want to follow but you have reached the 2,000 limit, you can go through those you are following and delete some that you no longer find interesting or relevant. Different rules apply to verified

accounts (those of famous people, indicated by a tick next to their username) – the general public cannot request verified accounts.

2 You can't follow people who have blocked you.

3 There is no limit to how many followers an account can have.

Direct messages can be sent only to a user who is following you. It's tantamount to saying that, by following you, they agree to be contacted by you (this is similar to Facebook with its pages and groups). If a user doesn't follow you, then you can't direct message them.

To follow a Twitter user, you simply hit 'Follow' on either their profile page or next to their username on search results. To encourage people to follow you, you need to post interesting, relevant tweets so the chances of getting retweets increase. The more retweets you get, the more Twitter users are likely to see your updates. You can also promote your Twitter account in other marketing (advertising, email signatures, business cards, etc.).

Try it now: Get following!

Log into your Twitter account and do a search for your competitors. Take a look at whom they are following and think about whether you should be following the same people. If yes, then go ahead and follow them! Follow the accounts for your local media outlets, too, and for any trade/sector publications, so that you can keep an eye out for anything relevant that you might be able to comment on.

Remember that others will look at the list of people you follow and make judgements about you based on that list. This might be another good reason for having both a personal and a professional Twitter account!

AVOID...

▶ **following just about anyone.** Make sure that the user is actually posting relevant information that is interesting to you.

Although around half of those you follow will follow you straight back, don't mass-follow everyone in the hope that your own number of followers will go up. It will clog up your timeline and you will have a large number of followers who aren't actually interested in you.

Posting tweets

As we pointed out in the introduction to this chapter, you have only 140 characters to get your message across. So, as with your bio, it's important to get to the point, and fast. It's even more difficult if you need to include a link or hashtag, as these deduct from the character count immediately. However, hashtags are important because they enable people who do not follow you to discover your tweets.

Again, try to avoid unnecessary textspeak; if you really are short of space, then use abbreviations, but don't overuse this style. Some people prefer to write in whole words but mark their tweets as [1/2] and [2/2], so their followers know that there's more to come, or that they have missed the first part. You don't need to worry about going over the limit, as Twitter and third-party apps display a character count near the space where you enter your update – the more letters you type, the more the 'characters remaining' count goes down. This is also handy as you can fiddle about with your update before you post it, ensuring that it fits within the limit but still makes sense!

Remember this: It's all public

Anything you post on Twitter can be seen by anyone with the URL to your profile or knowledge of your username. Alternatively, you can choose to 'protect' your tweets by checking a box in the 'Account' section of your profile settings. This means that no one can see your tweets unless you have accepted their request to follow you. Keep it all above board, as we discussed in Chapter 1, and you shouldn't have any problems.

Key idea: HTs, MTs and RTs

It's Twitter courtesy to acknowledge the source of your update rather than just copy and paste exactly what someone else has said. You can retweet another user simply by clicking the 'retweet' link under the update you want to share. Manually, you can copy and paste the update and add 'RT @username' to the beginning of it. You can also edit the tweet so that it's shorter or just contains the bit you think is most important. These kinds of updates should start 'MT @username' to show that you have modified a tweet from that user.

Finally, you can post a link, photo or update that contains something that was contained in another user's tweet by ending it 'HT @username'. If you are retweeting an update that contains a link, always make sure that the link actually works – there's no point retweeting a link that you haven't visited. Your followers will want to access this content.

AVOID...

▶ **retweeting everything!** You need to share your own views on Twitter, not everybody else's. People should be following you because they like what you have to say, not because you are sharing what other people have said. Your objective should be to have other people retweeting your tweets.

REPLYING

You can reply to any tweet you read by simply clicking the 'reply' link under that tweet. A box will automatically pop up containing the username of the account that sent the tweet you are replying to. All that's left to do is enter the reply you want to send them.

TIME

You may find that you just don't have the time to either post tweets or respond to those who are tweeting you. Alternatively, you might find Twitter addictive. For either situation, you may find it helpful to delegate the task to a colleague. Make sure they understand what they are and are not allowed to post.

They need to understand the role fully or they will either post anything or not enough. Give them the authorization to respond to others on behalf of your project but make it clear that, if they have any doubts, they should refer back to you.

Most of all, your tweets must appear authentic. You will quickly lose followers if people think you are no longer sending your own tweets.

An alternative to delegating is to use a third-party Twitter app such as Hootsuite or TweetDeck. Both of these allow you to queue updates so that you don't have to be online to tweet at a particular time. You can write the update and then specify the time and date that you would like that update to be posted. This is also a good thing to look into if Twitter distracts you – using a third-party app to queue your posts means that you don't have to look at the site very often. However, there is much more to Twitter than simply sending tweets. You need to keep track of what those who are following you are saying, too.

For more information about TweetDeck and HootSuite, take a look at Chapter 4.

Other features of Twitter

ADDING IMAGES

All you need to do to add an image to your tweet is to click the small camera icon that displays on twitter.com when you go to write an update. You will then need to browse the files on your computer until you find the image you want to share. A link will be generated to display that image when a user clicks on it. Twitter will take the character length of this link out of your 140 limit.

The photo you want to include must be less than 3 megabytes in size. Gif, jpeg and png are the only supported file types. You can upload only one image per tweet in Twitter and the only way to delete them is to delete the tweet that contains them.

INSERTING LINKS

As some links can be really long and over 140 characters alone, a lot of Twitter users use link-shortening websites such as bit.ly or tiny.url to make the link shorter. You don't even have to sign up for an account with sites in order to use them – you just paste in the link you want to be shortened and, hey presto, it churns out the shorter version for you to paste into your Twitter update. If you are running a blog either on your website or separately on a different blog-hosting platform, you will want to tweet links to every new post that you publish.

HASHTAGS

These are an incredibly easy way to get a discussion going and to keep track of what people are saying. If you want to turn a phrase into a hashtag, putting the # sign in front of a word or phrase will turn it into a link – people can click that link to get updates from everyone on Twitter using the same hashtag. Popular hashtags can become trending topics if many people use them in their updates.

> **Remember this:** Making a hashtag
>
> For example, *#riotcleanup* works, but if you put *#riot* clean up, then the linked hashtag would just be the word 'riot'.

You can search for hashtags and save those searches for later. This means you can check periodically to see what is happening, and who is contributing to a subject you are particularly interested in. By including the hashtag in your own comment, others following the debate will be introduced to you and your views.

A very popular way that hashtags are used is to promote and monitor conversation at conferences and events. The conference organizer will use a hashtag to promote the event and encourage pre-conference debate. Then, by making sure there is Wi-Fi in the conference hall, they will encourage delegates to share their comments using Twitter and the conference hashtag. Monitoring the Twitter debate gives the organizer a feel for the mood of the conference. Moreover, it gives them soundbites they can use onstage and even identify people with an interesting point to make, and who can then be invited on to the stage to make it.

Try it now: Tweet with a hashtag

Take a look at some of the hashtags that organizations and projects in your sector are using. Is there something you could post using one of those hashtags? Is there a debate going on that you could join? If there's nothing that you can think of to post, write a general update that introduces your project to Twitter and include your location and a service as a hashtag. For example, 'New #gardening company serving #Manchester. Could we help tame that unruly garden? Visit website for more info!'

Remember this: Hashtags are public

Anyone can use your hashtag, regardless of whether or not it's for the purpose it started out with. Hashtags can do good (#riotcleanup) or bad (see #McDStories later in this chapter). There's nothing you can do to stop people hijacking your hashtag. The most you can do is learn from your mistakes, and start again with something different. Bear the following tips in mind:

* **Don't backtrack.** Once your campaign is launched, if things start going wrong you have just got to wait it out. Try to get it back to what you intended, but don't remove your tweets that contain the hashtag – this won't stop people using it and it won't remove any mentions; it's still going to be out there.

* **Avoid emotive topics.** If you face a topic head on that people feel strongly about, be prepared to be the focus of some of those strong feelings.

* **Keep it specific.** Keeping hashtags specific makes it difficult for others to use them for other things. People will have no choice but to use them in the way you want them to.

ON THE GO

It really is easy to update your followers with news as it happens if you have got the Twitter application installed on your smartphone. This is why Twitter is so popular at conferences and events – you can be sitting in on a seminar and tweeting feedback while you are still in the room. As mentioned, events often have their own hashtags so that people attending that event can discuss with each other their thoughts, even if they have never actually met before – and you won't need a computer to do so.

PROMOTED TWEETS

Promoted tweets are clearly set apart from regular tweets as they will be labelled as such. These are basically tweets that advertisers have paid to have appear in prominent positions. These tweets will appear at the top of searches that are relevant and also on home pages, even if a user doesn't follow that account, but it will only appear if it's relevant to them.

A promoted tweet will only appear once on a user's home page and it will scroll down with the rest of the tweets. Alternatively, a user can click the 'Dismiss' link under a promoted tweet and it will disappear from their timeline.

Let's do it now

Of necessity, this chapter so far has focused as much on *what* to write as it has on *how* to write. Let's now bring it all together and give you the opportunity to practise writing some tweets. Communicating your message in an interesting and perhaps humorous way, together with relevant names and links, all within a 140-character limit, is an art form in itself.

The difference between a good tweet and an outstanding tweet that is retweeted by many people is in the way it is written. Being factual or opinionated alone is not enough. Your tweets have to capture the essence of the point you are making in a memorable, entertaining and impactful way. It doesn't matter if your tweet is about a piece of news, a current hot topic or promoting a special offer, the techniques that can make it memorable will be the same.

Even something as short as a 140-character tweet should have **structure**. Each tweet should contain as many of these sections as possible, included in the order they are listed below:

1 **hook** – two or three words that say it all

2 **angle** – your take on the point or story

3 **link** – a hashtag or hyperlink to take you deeper into the story

4 **twist** – a piece of wordplay (or hashtag) that makes the tweet unique.

Imagine, for example, that you are tree surgeon looking to attract new customers. You have seen the thread developing on Twitter about strong winds. It uses the hashtag #gales and you decide to pitch in with an offer.

> Worried about #gales? Is there a branch a little too close to you? Have chainsaw, will travel! #cheaperthaninsuranceclaim

Analysing the tweet using our four-part structure, we have:

1 **hook** – Worried about #gales?

2 **angle** – Is there a branch a little too close to you? Have chainsaw, will travel!

3 **link** – your username (such as @treefeller99)

4 **twist** – #cheaperthaninsuranceclaim

By making the twist into a hashtag, you both reduce your character count (no spaces) and create impact as the viewer's eye is drawn to the hashtag phrase. Plus, of course, the hashtag you have created might just catch on to attract even more followers to your profile.

Case study: #McDStories

Not all Twitter campaigns involving hashtags have a happy ending, as McDonalds found out at the start of 2012. As we have learned, hashtags are a great way to get a conversation going among Twitter users and the fast-food company wanted to start its own.

It began with #MeetTheFarmers – a paid-for campaign to show the real-life people involved 'behind the scenes' in producing the food that McDonalds serves. Unfortunately, it wasn't long before McDonalds changed the hashtag to #McDStories, in an attempt to get others sharing their (positive) real-life stories about the franchise.

The hashtag became a *bashtag* and Twitter users were instead using it to share their negative experiences of McDonalds, letting others know about the poor service and bad food they had experienced.

On Twitter

Robert says...

I was a Twitter cynic until New Year's Day 2011. That morning I decided to make the effort to understand this bizarre abbreviated world of @ signs and # hashtags. It made little sense, yet folk were telling me how useful it had become. I simply couldn't see it.

But over time, it began to come clear. I read a few guides and these helped demystify the process. Writing this book with Jess has helped me learn even more; for example, I'd not used MT before and now I do.

Twitter is fast, frequent and gives me access to a world full of people I'd otherwise never meet. In fact, most I will never meet because they are too busy to stop and talk. But they do listen to Twitter and that's why it's so very powerful.

Hashtags enable me to find new people with a common interest. Use a conference hashtag and tweet controversially in the morning and you will soon find people to chat to over lunch. What's more, journalists use and attribute tweets as 'soundbites'; a good reason to tweet as yourself and not under some wacky pseudonym.

Twitter keeps you in touch. For me, when writing, I'll stumble across a really pithy, pertinent phrase. These I lift out of the manuscript and tweet straight away. These preview the coming book but, more importantly, form the thought-provoking content I know my Twitter followers want to read.

Jess says...

Having been solely a Facebook user before I started working for Robert, setting up a Twitter account felt weird and took a while to get the hang of. While I'm able to have two profiles, one for work and one for personal use, it's always at the back of my mind that without opting to protect my tweets they can be viewable by anyone.

I make it clear on my personal profile that it is just that, personal, and I even link to my work account so that business acquaintances can follow me there instead. My profile pictures and usernames for the two accounts are completely different, so I never muddle up the accounts and post to the wrong one.

Focus points

* Twitter allows for only 140 characters in a tweet – this means you have to be focused and to the point with your updates.
* Tweet only relevant and interesting information that people will want to read and retweet – users won't retweet something that they have found boring and irrelevant. Remember that retweeting helps on the path to gaining new followers.
* Keep a friendly and approachable tone when replying – don't provoke people who leave negative feedback and take matters private if it looks as if a situation will get out of control.
* Avoid slang and overuse of abbreviations. Although this is forgivable on Twitter given the character limit, don't use abbreviations for the sake of it. If you do have to use them, make sure they are understandable.
* Stick to the four main types of update – news, customer service, special offers and feedback.

Summary

Well done, if you have now set yourself up on Twitter and posted your first few tweets. You should also have started following users who work in the same field as you or who share an interest. Retweet the things they post occasionally if you think it will be interesting to those who follow you. Add relevant hashtags to your tweets to join in a discussion or get one started.

Remember to add your Twitter handle and a link to your profile to your email signature. Let your family and friends know that you are active on the site, as they will no doubt be more than happy to oblige by following you!

Next step

Now that we have covered Facebook and Twitter, there's just one social media giant left to tackle... LinkedIn!

LinkedIn

In this chapter you will learn:

▶ *how to set up on LinkedIn quickly and easily and create a professional profile*
▶ *how to network effectively*
▶ *how to use one of LinkedIn's most powerful features – groups.*

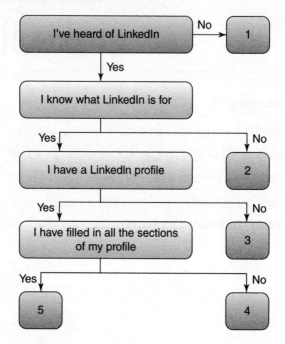

Self-assessment: What should I be using LinkedIn for?

Take the diagnostic test below and define your starting point for your journey through the LinkedIn network.

I've heard of LinkedIn — No → 1

Yes ↓

I know what LinkedIn is for

Yes ↓   No → 2

I have a LinkedIn profile

Yes ↓   No → 3

I have filled in all the sections of my profile

Yes ↓ 5   No → 4

Feedback

1 No problem – it's not as well known as Facebook and Twitter because it has a much more professional focus. In this chapter we will tell you everything you need to know.

2 We will cover what LinkedIn is for in depth; it's great for professionals looking to connect to other like-minded individuals and can lead to collaboration.

3 So you know what LinkedIn is but haven't got round to setting yourself up on there. Maybe you are not sure what the benefits could be for you? Read on to find out!

4 In this chapter we will describe what you need to write for each section of your profile and what main points you need to include.

5 You have set yourself up with a profile and filled in each section. But have you filled them in correctly? Take a look at our description of each section to check that you have included important points.

The new coffee shop

> 'All men are caught in an inescapable network of mutuality.'
>
> Martin Luther King, Jr. (1929–68)

Like it or not, we are all dependent upon each other. The world of work is, in reality, a complex web of connected people and organizations. In 18th-century London, business was done in coffee shops. What mattered most was to be seen, known and recognized for the abilities and contacts that you had. The coffee shop was also a place of debate. It's where the issues of the day were discussed and where groups of people with a common interest gathered to explore mutual opportunity.

Of course, coffee shops are also important today, but in modern times networks extend a lot further. The business world is more complicated, faster and global. The Internet allows us to communicate and build our own professional networks across national boundaries. The contemporary equivalent of the 18th-century coffee shop is a website called LinkedIn.

LinkedIn is very similar to Facebook in that you can profile yourself and build a network of connections. However, unlike Facebook, LinkedIn is always used to build professional rather than social networks. LinkedIn claims to be the world's largest professional network. It has more than 175 million members. It is undoubtedly the place to be, if you want to be seen by potential employers, employees, business partners and customers.

Background

LinkedIn launched in 2003 and has grown rapidly over the years, to include members in more than 200 countries. Around half its members are in the USA and there are more than 11 million users in Europe. As one might expect, the fastest growth of new membership is taking place in the emerging economies. This means that if you are looking to do business or grow your career in India, China or the Far East, then LinkedIn is perhaps the best way to make contact with the right people in the right countries.

LinkedIn illustrates well the way that the Internet has democratized business transactions. A few years ago, if you wanted to do business in another country, your starting point would be overseas trade missions and the embassy network. Today LinkedIn allows you easily to identify the people most likely to be helpful to you in the countries you want to target. You can contact them directly, as well as join groups and enter discussions on the professional topics that interest you most.

This is the online equivalent of going to the right coffee shop, frequented by the right group of people, in the right part of town. The difference, of course, is that LinkedIn enables you to filter out exactly the people you need to meet. It also means that you can contact them easily and readily without the need to be in the same place at the same time. LinkedIn takes away the guesswork and uncertainty of professional networking.

Why use LinkedIn?

LinkedIn is perfect for growing your reputation and professional network, and also becoming known and respected in your business field. LinkedIn is also perfect for growing your career, because you will list your CV on your profile and invite people who have worked with you to post testimonials. This means that somebody looking for a particular skill set or specific past experience can not only find you, but also find out how others value the work that you have done.

The more specific you make your targeting, the more successful you will be. Indeed, if you try to connect with too many people with whom you have too little in common, you may find your LinkedIn account blocked. People have the opportunity to complain about unwelcome invitations to connect. This facility maintains what might be called 'professional standards' of conduct on the LinkedIn platform.

THINGS TO AVOID

≫ In many walks of life, both online and in the real world, the boundaries between social and professional interaction are blurred. On Facebook, for example, it is not unusual for people to mix business postings with social comment on their profile. This would not be a good idea on LinkedIn.

≫ It is also wise to avoid arguments and criticism when posting comments on LinkedIn groups. You will see this happen often as people become irritated by, or perhaps simply misunderstand, what others are writing. You will sometimes see quite complicated arguments developing into major rows between otherwise very professional people over points of detail.

≫ As with all online communication, it is simply not as clear as the spoken word. When a group of people have a conversation on a LinkedIn group, it is very different from having that same conversation in a room. Avoid being drawn into an argument and instead always assume the positive and err on the side of caution.

In the summer of 2012, LinkedIn:

▶ had more than 175 million users in more than 200 countries worldwide

▶ had massive market penetration in some countries – for example, it is estimated that 30 per cent of professional people in the Netherlands are on LinkedIn

▶ grew the fastest among professionals living and working in the emerging economies of India, China, South America and the Far East

▶ saw traffic to its website increase by more than 60 per cent year on year.

Signing up

If you have yet to sign up with LinkedIn, let's start building your profile right now. Go to the LinkedIn home page (linkedin.com) and click to create a new account. Remember to create a password which is both difficult for others to guess and easy for you to remember. It is unlikely that others will hijack your LinkedIn profile, but it is good practice to make this as difficult as possible to happen.

Try it now: Look at others' profiles

Take a look at the profiles of people you know well and see how they are written. Make a note of the things you like about other people's profiles and also the things you do not. As with any form of business writing, it is always good to start by looking at what others have done before writing anything of your own.

Finally, please bear in mind that LinkedIn uses keywords in the same way as Facebook to help people find the right people when they search. You won't be asked to list keywords separately, so be sure to embed the most important words within the copy that you write. For example, if you are a specialist in craniofacial reconstructive surgery, you need to say this rather than just describing yourself as a plastic surgeon.

Your profile

Once you have created your account, your first task should be to build your profile. This is essentially your online CV, so you may need to have handy any earlier CVs you have written, perhaps for job applications. That way, you will have a useful aide-memoire of the things you have done and the dates when you did them.

Remember this: It's like your CV

As with any CV, your LinkedIn profile should not have gaps. The art of writing your LinkedIn profile is not to conceal the roles about which you are least proud, but to present everything in as positive a way as possible.

Let's now look at each section of the profile in turn:

SUMMARY

The summary of your LinkedIn profile should be similar to the opening paragraph on the CV. It should describe in fewer than 100 words what you do, how you are different and what most of all will encourage people to contact you. Here is the summary from my (Robert's) own LinkedIn profile to show you what I mean:

> The focus of my work is social entrepreneurship and how this can liberate, empower individuals, organizations and communities. I'm a popular speaker, able to help people see the real opportunities behind the Big Society rhetoric.

> My twelfth book *How to be a Social Entrepreneur* was described by the *Guardian* as 'comprehensive and easy to read'.

> I work best with organizations wrestling with a funding conundrum. I have the creativity, experience, tact and contacts to usually find a solution.

Let me explain each of the three sections in a little more detail:

▶ First, I explain what I do and emphasize the fact that I am a popular conference speaker. I have done this because conference speaking is the most lucrative work that I do. It is also a good way to meet new consultancy clients.

- ▶ Second, I differentiate myself from everybody else who claims to be an expert in my field. The fact that I am an established author suggests that I know my subject. Just in case that is not enough, the quote from the *Guardian* provides a useful third-party endorsement.

- ▶ Finally, I include a call to action. What exactly is the most common challenge facing the person looking at my profile? I have tried to summarize this in a way that will encourage people to make contact, to ask for more information about the way I work.

I update my profile regularly and you should do the same.

EXPERIENCE

At first glance, this section is just the same as an online CV. Indeed, it does allow you to list all of your career positions, from college to the present. But it also allows you to list concurrent roles. In other words, if you are a senior manager in a horticultural business, on the board of a national trade association and a governor of your local high school, you can list each of these as current positions.

Because your profile will show your three most recent positions first, people viewing your profile will see a bigger picture than would be portrayed simply by a description of your day job. Having a national industry leadership role suggests you are better connected and a more strategic thinker than if you simply worked in your job and then went home and watched TV. The same is true of a community role because it demonstrates that you are a more rounded and engaged individual.

It doesn't matter whether you are looking to be headhunted, or simply want to recruit more customers to your organization, the more significant you appear on your LinkedIn profile the more attractive you will become to people, who might well be able to help you in the future.

Try to write your description of each role as succinctly as possible. Use the same three-section rule that we applied to your summary. Try to avoid simply listing all the things that you do, unless, that is, you work in a highly technical field where this is relevant.

Make sure that you end your description of each role in a way that makes it obvious why you moved on to the thing you did next. It may be that redundancy forced you from regular employment to life as a freelancer, but this should be described as a positive life-changing opportunity, not a damning indictment on that stage of your career.

EDUCATION

The education section can be quite difficult to complete. This is particularly true if you are older and perhaps did not go to university. I, for example, achieved an HND in Agriculture in 1978 and have gained no academic qualification since. Of course, I have done an awful lot of learning over the ensuing 35 years, but the LinkedIn profile does not enable me to make that point.

If you look at my LinkedIn profile, you will see I have put very little in the education section. If you are older and successful in your field, this section of your profile is the least important. If, on the other hand, you are younger and in the early stages of your career, having and listing a good selection of academic qualifications will be very important indeed.

Complete this section honestly and, if in doubt, leave it blank.

ADDITIONAL INFORMATION

You will be surprised how many people add links to websites in this section that do not work. If you wish to link to a number of websites, it is helpful to say what each of them are. To be confronted with a choice of three 'company website' links is not helpful.

You can also add links to any blogs you may have and, most importantly, a link to your Twitter account. (You can also connect your Twitter feed to your LinkedIn profile so that your tweets appear on the right-hand side of your LinkedIn profile.)

Finally, there is an opportunity to list your interests, which I suggest should be work-related and simple; groups and associations of which you are a member; and any honours or awards you have received.

Because this section appears at the very bottom of your profile, it is remarkably easy to forget to keep it up to date. Make a diary note to review and check your LinkedIn profile every month. You will be surprised how quickly things change and how easy it is to keep your profile current when you do this as a matter of habit.

PHOTOGRAPH

LinkedIn allows you to upload a photograph to illustrate your profile. It won't be very large and so should primarily be a head-and-shoulders image.

You want people to be able to print out your profile, take it to an event and recognize you from across the room. Try to avoid adding a passport-style photograph taken in one of those photo booths at your local railway station. For this, and any other business use, it is vitally important to have a small portfolio of professionally taken business-related portraits. My advice is always to pay a professional photographer to take some images of you in your workplace at least once every couple of years.

By using the same photograph across all of your social media platforms, as well as on your personal or business website, you begin to build your personal brand. For example, I never wear a tie and mostly wear a collarless shirt, even on the most formal business occasions. My profile photographs are therefore always informal because that reflects my style of work.

If the work that you do means that you would normally dress in a certain way, or carry certain items of equipment, then these could be included in your profile photograph. For example, if you are a doctor, having a stethoscope around your neck would mean that people could see that you are doctor at first glance, before they read a single word of your profile.

Try it now: Complete your profile

Using the tips I have mentioned above, get stuck into editing your profile. You can always come back to amend it later when you think of something else to add.

Building your network

You will already know lots of people with LinkedIn profiles. But unless you have spent time searching LinkedIn, you won't know which of your contacts are already there. Luckily, LinkedIn makes it easy for you to cross-reference your existing network with LinkedIn. Once you have created your profile, you can import your email contacts and let LinkedIn check to see who has a profile already.

LinkedIn then gives you a list of your existing contacts who already have LinkedIn profiles. You can then choose those you would like to be connected with in your new network. Finally, you simply click on a button to 'invite selected contacts' and the invitations are automatically sent.

You can also search for people you know, using the search panel at the top right of your LinkedIn screen. This can be great fun but actually has a serious application. When you encounter someone you know, or perhaps are to meet for the first time, checking their LinkedIn profile can give you an insight into their career and specialisms.

Finally, if you have listed the organizations you have worked for and colleges you have attended, you can click on those to discover other people who have those organizations in common with you. Some you will already know and others, perhaps, might be useful to know.

As a rule of thumb, on LinkedIn you only connect with people with whom you have an existing connection. To speculatively approach someone you do not know goes against the unspoken protocol of LinkedIn. You do have an opportunity to add a message to your invitation to connect. The skill with which you write this message will dictate your success in linking with a relative stranger.

Remember this: Quality over quantity

Anthropologists tell us that our brains can really only handle a network of around 150 close contacts. Every time a nomadic tribe of early humans grew to about 150 members, it would split to form two tribes.

LinkedIn enables you to build a business tribe of many thousands. However, the more people you add to your network the less well you will be able to keep in touch with and know the individuals within it. It is useful to ask yourself how many people you need to know to build a career or business that you want.

Be selective and don't be afraid to remove people from your network to keep the numbers manageable.

INVITING SOMEONE YOU DO NOT KNOW TO CONNECT ON LINKEDIN

At the top left-hand corner of each profile is a blue box which says 'Connect'. Click on this and your invitation to that person is on your screen. You have to tick a box to say whether you consider the person to be one of the following –colleague, classmate, we have done business together, friend, other, or I don't know the person.

My personal choice, if approaching someone I do not really know, is to tick the box that says 'We have done business together'. I then use the personal note below to explain why we haven't done business together yet but might do soon!

The personal note gives you the following text automatically:

> I'd like to add you to my professional network on LinkedIn.
>
> – your name

If you want the person to accept your invitation, you need to add a more compelling reason than that provided by default. You need to get this message across in very few words. The recipient may spend only a few seconds looking at your invitation before deciding whether to accept or ignore it.

Here are some examples I have used myself:

> I'd like to add you to my professional network on LinkedIn. I really enjoyed your presentation at the conference yesterday and hope by connecting here I can learn more from your work.
>
> Robert Ashton

I'd like to add you to my professional network on LinkedIn. I am already a supporter of the charity you run and would really like to get more involved.

Robert Ashton

I'd like to add you to my professional network on LinkedIn. Jessica Juby has been promising to introduce us for some time, so I thought I would take the lead. I see from your profile that we share an interest in classic tractors. Perhaps we should meet and compare notes?

Robert Ashton

In each example I have kept the original text and simply added to it. This works for me but may not work for you so well. If you plan to make a lot of approaches via LinkedIn, you might do things differently. Imagine you are a recruitment consultant planning to use LinkedIn to find candidates. You might then build your own collection of introductory paragraphs. Keep them handy on a Word file and then copy, paste and edit them into LinkedIn each time you need to use them.

Try it now: Make your first connection

Find someone on LinkedIn that you have worked with and invite them to connect with you. Remember to add a personal invitation to remind them of who you are.

Key idea: Degrees of separation

It is said that no two people in the world are separated by more than six connected individuals. LinkedIn exploits that chain of contacts by identifying contacts of contacts. When you look at the profile page of one of your contacts, you will see to the right of their name a small blue box which contains the text '1st'. This is because that person is separated from you by just 1 degree. If you then click on that person's list of contacts, you will see that each has '2nd' next to their name. And if you click on the contacts of one of these people you will see '3rd'.

Perhaps somebody is connected with three of your contacts but not with you, so LinkedIn will suggest them as contacts to you. This can be a really useful way of discovering new people to whom you can readily be introduced by people you know. The more you are connected with the people outside your immediate network, the faster your network will grow.

In fact, the best way to grow your network is to ask the people you know to make an introduction via LinkedIn. You do this by scrolling to the bottom of their profile and clicking on 'get introduced through a connection'. You will have a list of shared connections from which you can choose the person you feel is most likely to make the introduction for you.

LinkedIn groups

One of the key strengths of LinkedIn is that it has a vast number of groups. These are special-interest forums where you can discuss topics of common interest with others. You will find a directory of groups by clicking on the word 'groups' in the LinkedIn toolbar.

Not all groups are active but LinkedIn helpfully tells you how many members each group has and how many discussions have taken place in the current month. These are good indicators of the popularity and activity of each group.

As your LinkedIn presence grows, the site will suggest groups you might like to join. It does this by identifying groups to which many of your contacts belong. You can also start groups and invite people to join them. However, it is usually better to join an existing group and become active within it than to start a new one and try to build membership.

As with all online writing, your contribution to group discussions on LinkedIn should be concise, relevant and positive. Remember that this is primarily a professional forum. Jocular banter of the kind you might indulge in on your Facebook page is probably not appropriate here on LinkedIn.

When you are a member of a LinkedIn group, you can:

- start a discussion about a topic you think will be of interest to others

- contribute to existing discussions started by other people

- comment on a particular point made by someone within a discussion

- show your approval for a point someone is making by 'liking' it.

HOW TO WRITE GROUP POSTS

Contributing to a group discussion is rather like having a conversation. The difference, of course, is that you are not all in the same room at the same time. This means you have to work harder to give the conversation focus and flow. Remember how annoying it is when you say something to somebody and their response shows clearly that they have not really been listening at all.

In a bad conversation, each participant has a series of points they want to get across. They wait until a pause and then leap in to make their point without any recognition of the points that have been made thus far. It happens most frequently when you are trying to buy something. The salesperson is more interested in describing the features of what they are selling than listening to you.

There are a number of techniques you can use to make sure that, when you are engaged in an online conversation, you make it clear that you are 'listening' to what is being said by others. The best way, though, is by repeating what someone has just said back to them. This is as true in an online discussion as face to face. You start your reply with a summary of what the other person has said. If you want to see this being done, look at a TV interview. Inevitably, the interviewee will start their answer by repeating the question asked by the interviewer. But you are writing online and so need to adapt this technique to work in a virtual environment.

Here is an example to illustrate the point. Imagine that you are a member of a LinkedIn group for people wishing to improve their public speaking. The discussion is opened by someone else who writes:

> I find it difficult to complete my presentations within the time allocated at a conference. This means I often have to rush the last few slides and fail to make the most important point well. Does anyone have any good tips to offer that might help me?

What is good about this opening is that a question is asked. Remember that people will be more likely to answer a question than simply respond to a comment. So now you want to answer the question and in doing so illustrate how you have conquered the challenge shared by the questioner. You write:

> I also have had this problem in the past. What has helped me is writing on my notes the times that I expect to reach each key point. I will write the time my presentation is due to start at the top of the first page. Then, when I rehearse the talk, I write the target arrival time at each key point, making sure that I have plenty of time to emphasize the final, most important point on which I plan to close. I hope this technique can help others.

Your reply has made a number of points very clear. The first is that you have experienced the same problem. The second, more importantly, is that you have taken the question seriously and are therefore showing some empathy with the questioner. Thirdly, you offered a solution which has worked for you. Your willingness to share information will suggest to others that you are a generous and nice person.

You could, for example, have said:

> I also have had this problem in the past and have developed some techniques which meant I always completed my presentation bang on time. These techniques are at the very heart of my 'be a better speaker' training program. You can buy a copy of my training DVD by clicking on this link.

This reply offers no practical help at all. Instead, you have offered to sell a training course which may or may not help the individual. While the first answer is clearly written to help someone, the second is written to help you and you alone.

You will find, as you take part in discussions on LinkedIn groups, that many people use them to sell themselves or the services of their organization. This is not the best way to build your reputation or profile on LinkedIn. The paradox is that the more people give freely to others the more popular and successful they will become. People will always choose to do business with people who give as much as they seek to gain.

Case study: Matthew Draycott (www.mdraycott.com)

Matthew is currently the Enterprise and Employability Development Officer at the University of East Anglia. This is just one line on his CV, though, as his LinkedIn profile shows.

Anyone interested in finding out more about Matthew can easily visit his profile to get a good, solid idea of his skills and experience. Making the most of the sections and features available, Matthew has filled out his profile using as much detail as possible.

You can find out about his current and past employment; read a summary of his skills and expertise; browse a list of his personal interests; and see a list of the universities he has graduated from. Taking it to a higher level, he even links to his publications and gives details of awards and nominations he has received.

'For me the value of LinkedIn isn't just about having my CV online; it's a powerful tool to connect me to other people through individuals in my existing networks, allowing me to showcase my skills and experience with testimonials that support my claims. It offers a functionality that is hard to find anywhere else on the Web. I also make a lot of use of groups to promote my ideas, projects and events to people outside my networks, allowing me to build new bridges.'

He knows the benefit of having his LinkedIn profile linking to other online portals – he links to his blog, project websites, social media accounts and PowerPoint slide collections via plugins. He keeps them all up to date following his personal online branding strategy to ensure they all present him in a consistent, professional way.

On LinkedIn

Robert says...

Before meeting anyone new, I check them out on LinkedIn. I want to know how they describe their current role, how long they have held it and what they have done before. I also want to know what others have said about them and whom we might know in common. LinkedIn gives me all that information on one page.

Because I know people do the same before meeting me, I make sure my profile is up to date. I make sure that people I work with, or who hear me speak, have every encouragement to post a recommendation. I must confess that, at times, I write these for them, although not very often!

For those in paid employment, LinkedIn is a living CV. For those working for themselves, it's a CV too.

LinkedIn groups are also great places to meet new people, although the discussions can become time-consuming and, at times, esoteric. In all walks of life, there are people who seem to have all the time in the world to write lengthy group posts and others with time to read them. I do take part, but mostly limit my comments to one or two lines.

LinkedIn is the most serious place I live online. But that's not to say it doesn't have humour, too. As in everything else, I simply say it as I see it and some find that amusing!

Jess says...

I'll admit that I'm not on the LinkedIn bandwagon yet – for me, personally, it has nothing to offer. As an employee in a very small company where, as an individual, I rarely do external work, there isn't any reason why people should want to connect with me on a social media site that is purely professional.

I've had one previous position that I held only for one season before joining Robert, so I don't have anyone to give recommendations to or receive them from. I dare say that, if I ever found myself in the position of needing to look for another job or expanding my current work position, then I'd probably have an increased interest in the site, but right now I'm focusing on Twitter and Facebook.

Focus points

✳ LinkedIn is purely for professional purposes. What you can get away with posting on Facebook won't usually be tolerated here.

✳ Your profile should successfully sell you as a professional. The better you describe your skills and experience, the more successful you will be in making new connections.

✳ You can grow your network through the people you already know by the 'degrees of separation' feature which introduces you to contacts of contacts.

✳ Contribute to groups and discussions to share your experience and knowledge with others, to help improve the impression your contacts, and contacts of contacts, have of you.

✳ Most recruitment companies use LinkedIn to search for suitable candidates. If you want to get on in your career, getting on LinkedIn will be a smart move.

Summary

You should now have set yourself up with a LinkedIn profile, if you didn't have one already, and have edited each section so that they each contain important information that will sell you. You have learned that your profile needs to be updated regularly.

Next step

Now that you have successfully wrestled with the three major online networks you should be a part of, it's time to look at blogging.

Blogging

In this chapter you will learn:

- ► *the terminology of blogging*
- ► *how to set up a blog, using a platform such as WordPress*
- ► *about the importance of your blog's credibility and how to gain that credibility*
- ► *how to win an audience for your blog and keep it, too*
- ► *the importance of building up a relationship with your readers, for example through comments.*

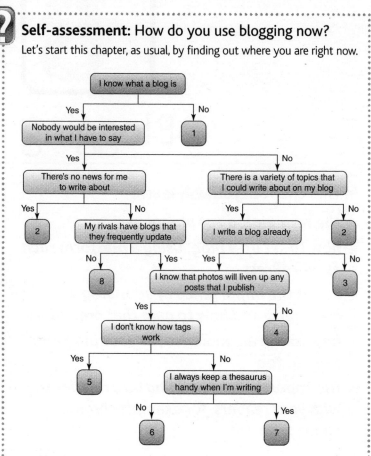

Feedback

1 We will give you a definition for the term 'blog' shortly. It's almost like an online diary but one that is open to everyone to read, so it's up to you to decide how personal the content is!

2 There doesn't need to be any news about your project for you to write about – you could write an article about something you have heard and want to share your feelings on. We will cover the different things you could write about further on in the chapter.

3 If you haven't got a blog, refer back to the WordPress instructions we went through in Chapter 3 on setting up a website. While it works

well for those who want quick and simple websites, WordPress is first and foremost a blogging platform.

4   If you have got photos or pictures you can use alongside a blog post, they will help to break up big chunks of text and bring some colour to the page. Keep reading to find out why it's important not to make your blog appear dull.

5   It's OK if you don't know how tags work; while we touched on these in the website chapter, we will cover them in more depth here. Similar to keywords, they help your blog posts to be found – read on for more information!

6   This is good. Always write whatever comes naturally; having to research for a better word isn't natural. You have made a good start to blogging – read on to pick up some tips on how to improve!

7   If you have to research a word, it's the wrong one. This chapter will highlight some other dos and don'ts for your blogging that will make it much more appealing to your readers and more fun for you to write.

8   If your competitors aren't blogging, then doing so yourself will distinguish you from the others and make you unique. You can lead the pack rather than follow it!

Sharing experience, knowledge and opinion

'One of the hardest things in life is having words in your heart that you can't utter.'

J. Earl Jones

Blogging has become one of the most personal ways you can communicate with others online. For some, it is a window on to their soul, being the place they share their innermost thoughts. For others, it's a way to express what they feel is right or wrong in the sector they work in, or the place they live. A blog is a great place to share – with those who are eager to learn – the experience and knowledge you accumulate as you grow in your position.

But blogging is not just about catharsis. Blogging is about being *read* – because when your blog is read, it can change attitudes, perceptions and behaviours. In other words, a good blog has the potential to change the world and your life.

The popular 2009 comedy drama film *Julie and Julia*, which starred Meryl Streep, was the first film to be based on a blog. Julie Powell was a young budding writer in New York who decided to cook every recipe in Julia Child's classic *Mastering the Art of French Cooking* and record the experience in a blog. First the blog became very popular and then it was adapted into the film.

It is unlikely that your blog will end up as a film. But it will stand no chance at all unless you make a start. This chapter will help you make a start and become a confident and competent blogger.

Terminology

Blogroll A feature of some but not all blogging platforms that allows you to list other blogs that you recommend people follow.

Categories Broad themes or topics that your posts are assigned under, to make them easier to find.

Comments The feedback that your blog readers can leave under each post.

RSS Feed RSS stands for Really Simple Syndication. This is the subscription service that allows people to sign up to receive your new content directly on to their home page or even by email.

Sidebar The left- and/or right-hand side panels on either side of your main page content that contain menu links and other widgets.

Tags You acknowledge the key terms and topics in your blog by assigning them as 'tags'. These help the posts to be found in relevant searches on search engines and also by readers on your blog looking to find more content on the same subject.

Benefits

There are a number of benefits for both you and your project from writing a blog. With a blog you can:

▶ **gather feedback from customers.** You can even get readers to participate in market research by posting polls and surveys.

▶ **develop a new income stream** by charging readers to view new posts. This won't be possible for all blogging platforms and only seasoned bloggers will be able to justify setting a fee, although most can generate some advertising income.

▶ **position yourself as an expert** and respected commentator in your sector by publishing informative posts that demonstrate your experience and knowledge in your field. You will find that the more you write, the more followers and respect you will collect.

▶ **increase your listings in search engine results.** Search engines love sites that frequently publish new content, which is exactly what blogs do (if you are maintaining it properly). This means that each new post is indexed by engines as a new possible result in a search, increasing the number of times your blog could appear in results. Each new tag that you use on your blog widens the number of search phrases a search engine can list you for. Search engines also show preference for sites that have been linked back to by other sites. Each new blog post can potentially be linked to from other sites and increases how search-engine friendly your blog is.

- ▶ **increase the amount of traffic to your website,** whether your blog is under the same domain, or separate if it's very search-engine friendly (as above).

- ▶ **build an audience.** These are the readers that will keep coming back to your blog or subscribe to receive new content, so it's vital to publish content that people want to read. Eventually, these people may become interested in working with you or supporting you in some other way.

- ▶ **build trust with your readers** by letting them get to know you. However, it is important to maintain boundaries between your personal and professional lives. Too much personal content on a professional blog can put people off.

Try it now: Research blogs in your sector

Spend a few minutes searching for blogs that are relevant to your sector or on a subject you are passionate about. Jot down a few notes that will influence your own blog. The questions in the following flow chart will help you put together a brief for the blog that you want to read. This will be an improvement on those that are out there because you will include anything that's missing or improve features that don't work.

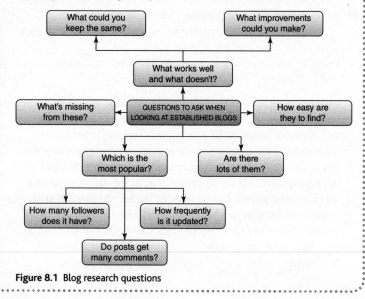

Figure 8.1 Blog research questions

Getting started

You may have some concerns about what you would write for your blog – you need to choose a subject that you can write about confidently and frequently. A topic that's too narrow won't give you enough to write about and one that's too broad won't make you focused enough, running the risk of you losing direction.

It really is all about targeting. Not only does your subject need to be one about which you are passionate, but that passion needs to be shared by other people, too. For example, if you were a keen gardener, blogging about gardening in general would make it difficult to build an audience. If your specialism in the garden, for example, is the South American flowering bulb, your subject might be too narrow. Bulb growing, however, might be where you need to be.

Blogging about a topic that you think will attract an audience, without sufficient knowledge or experience of that topic, will be neither sustainable nor successful. This can be a problem when people decide to develop an interest in something they see to be very lucrative. As a rule, you will do better to focus on what you know best and then use your knowledge and enthusiasm to encourage others to share the interest with you.

Before you set out to start your own blog, it can be a good idea to test the waters first by writing a guest blog (or several!) for an already established blog.

Key idea: Try guest blogging

An established blogger may choose to let other writers submit articles to be published on their blog. They have to follow the same theme of the blog but these posts bring a fresh viewpoint to the blog and will liven it up with a change of tone and style. The owner of the blog can decide not to publish a piece, though, if they feel it doesn't fit comfortably within the blog parameters that they have already set.

Alternatively, when your own blog is set up, it's a great opportunity to invite people who are well known in your chosen sector to contribute to your blog. You can then publicize their involvement through Twitter and Facebook, to encourage their followers to follow you as well.

Remember this: Remember to sign off

Whenever writing any kind of online article for someone else or a website that's not yours, always remember to include a little bit about you at the bottom of the article. Include a very brief sentence about you or what you do and definitely make sure to include a link back to your own website. This is called a byline.

Alternatively, you may already have been a guest blogger and now want to get set up on your own, or feel ready to take that leap.

SETTING UP YOUR BLOG

There are many different blogging platforms out there. They all work in similar ways, but they look different and have a few different features. Blogger (www.blogger.com), Tumblr (www.tumblr.com) and WordPress (www.wordpress.com) are three to note, but, to keep things simple, because we have already covered WordPress in our website chapter, this is the platform we will be sticking to.

Try it now: Start your blog

If you have decided to go ahead and start your own blog, that's great. Head over to Chapter 2, which lists the instructions for setting up a blog with WordPress. To keep your blog very simple, you can have just one static page on which your posts will be published.

YOUR PROFILE

This can serve as a handy introduction to your blog. It can sit on a static page. Your profile can then introduce your blogs, which will be listed beneath it. You will need to include a paragraph giving an overview of your blog – what aims and themes does it have? Write a couple of lines about why the blog was started, who the contributors are, and why they are involved.

Your readers will want to know what it is that motivates you or what experience you have that gives you the authority to write about your chosen subject area. You may also want to briefly cover any guidelines for comments or guest blogs if you are willing to consider them for publication.

The golden rule of business blogging is to make your writing style very personal, but without writing about personal things. In other words, a blog should have a friendly, conversational style, rather than being formal and potentially stilted. It's OK to write about how you feel about your subject because this is relevant and may be similar to the feelings your blog prompts in the mind of your reader. But draw the line before including anecdotes or revelations about your personal life.

Posting

Now that you have decided whether to guest blog or write for your own blog, it's time to take a closer look at how to write your posts. Refer back to the sections on writing etiquette and standards in Chapter 1.

The majority of blogging platforms will allow you to 'queue' posts so that you can write them when you have time and set them to be published at a later date.

Credibility

For your blog to attract and retain readers, it has to be credible. There are several things you can do for each post to ensure they stay credible:

▶ **Reference source material correctly,** quoting anything that is not originally yours. Set references out in the following way:

'article title', author, location of article, date.

For example:

'View from the motorcade', Robert Ashton, civilsociety. co.uk, 2012.

- **Don't attempt to stuff keywords into articles** – if they didn't naturally flow into the article, you shouldn't force them in. (WordPress, for example, enables you to list keywords in a separate box underneath your article.) It doesn't matter how well the keywords fit the style of the blog; they are there to help both reader and search engines signpost your post.

- **If you are being paid to advertise a product,** make it clear to your audience that it's a paid advertisement. Not doing so is misleading.

- **Be impartial and fair** when writing reviews and giving your opinion.

- **Avoid typographical errors.** Proofread your articles before they 'go live' to check that they flow nicely and that you have not made any spelling mistakes. Most blogging platforms have built-in spellcheckers in their editors so these should be flagged up. (However, spellchecking will not pick up grammatical errors.) Finally, read your blog again once published, and reopen and edit if you spot errors at this stage.

- **Follow the writing standards and etiquette** we outlined in Chapter 1 of this book – your writing will be so much better for it.

Remember this: Be consistent

All your posts must support the same overall message. Your followers will have subscribed to you because they want to read more from you on this topic. If you switch topic, you risk alienating your audience and losing readers. It might help to think of your blog as an organization. Give it a mission and perhaps even define that mission in the opening blog. Then check each post to make sure it fits well with the overall mission of the blog before you post. This will prevent you from drifting off course over time.

Hyperlinks

We have covered hyperlinks in more detail in Chapter 3, but these are the main points you need to know:

- All hyperlinks should be set to open in a new window, so that your visitors aren't taken completely away from your website.

- You should check all hyperlinks within an article before making it live, to ensure that the links actually work.

- Don't use excess words to introduce hyperlinks – embed them within text you have already written.

- Don't overuse hyperlinks – make sure they are relevant and necessary.

Audience

Tagging your posts correctly will draw in a large part of your audience. Some of your readers will also reblog your content to their own sites and some well-established sites may even post a link to your post if they think it's good enough and relevant to their own readers.

You need to make sure that, every time you post a new blog, you share it on whatever social media channels you are signed up to: tweet a shortened link to your Twitter account followers and share it on your Facebook timeline, to encourage your members or fans to take a look. This will also allow those connected to you to share on their own accounts and the link can then spread to many different accounts.

Your first post

Whether your first post is for someone else's blog or your own, it can often help to ask someone else to read it through before you submit or publish it. This is particularly true if you have laboured long and hard over crafting your post. Sometimes, the more you edit a piece of writing, the less understandable it becomes. Make sure you choose someone who fits within your target audience. Then their feedback will be far more beneficial than if you have chosen someone who just knows you – for example your partner, a colleague or your mum! It's important to get your first post just right, as it will set the tone for future posts.

A lot of people choose to use their first post as an introduction to them, their work and what the blog will be about. This prevents you getting to the detail of your blog's message. That said, it can be a nice way to ease into the blog – both for you and your readers.

For those who are used to writing and have confidence, blogging will come easily. But if this is not you, do not be worried by others you know who seem to dive straight in and produce good articles without, seemingly, any effort at all. It is a good idea to sketch out the key points you want to make before starting. If you aim to expand each point into a paragraph, your writing will flow in a logical way towards the conclusion you want to make.

YOUR TOPIC

The first important thing to decide on is a topic. What will your first blog post be about? You may decide to give an overall introduction to your blog's message, aiming to address finer points in later posts.

The headline of your post will be the first thing that draws a reader in; you have then got to make sure you keep their attention in the introduction and the following sections. Play around with some possible post titles – the title should indicate what the post is about without going into detail (and not using too many words!) and also capture the attention of the reader to invite them to read further. Word it so that some keywords are included, but don't force them in.

It will help you to formulate your headline if you have decided on the key conclusion you want to draw at the end of your posting. As with your tweets, wordplay will also help you formulate a memorable headline. As a rule of thumb, always try to capture your key point in both the headline and closing paragraph. Using some of the same words will help.

THE STRUCTURE

Next, you will need to write the introduction. Here, it's crucial to tell the reader why it's important that they read this article. Capture their attention and show them the benefits of the article, to keep them reading on. Think of this paragraph as a fishing hook and your headline as bait. One attracts your reader and the other keeps them engaged.

If you have a lot you want to say (and don't feel that it's better to split this into a series of posts), you can continue by bullet-pointing the different key points you want to cover. Expand on each of these points with fuller sentences, which will form the main body of your post.

Think about whether you have any images you could use in your post to liven it up. You must have permission to publish photos that aren't owned by you. (In particular, you can get into trouble for copying and reusing photographs published by newspapers.) However, there are several websites out there that have stock photos for download either for free or for a nominal charge. www.stockvault.net is one that has free images. Some photographers will request that you credit them when using their images – the best way to do this is to put a sentence at the end of your blog that simply says 'Image(s) supplied by [*name*].'

When you have finished writing the main body of your article, you will need to round it off with a conclusion. You must include a summary of your main points and a call to action. What do you want the reader to do as a result of reading your blog post? It's best to tie in your conclusion with your introduction – what benefits of reading the article did you outline there? Reiterate them here to really make them hit home.

Your post will have more credibility if the conclusion it draws is not overtly something that benefits you or your organization. For example, you may work for a company that sells equity release schemes to older people. Your blog might highlight some of the dangers of setting the scheme up with an unscrupulous provider. It would be appropriate for the conclusion to be that the buyer and their family check what is offered against a list of criteria you provide in the blog. Naturally, your firm would meet all those criteria. But to write a conclusion saying that buying from you is the best option would make the blog appear to be nothing more than advertising.

The very last thing you will need to do before publishing any article on your blog is to read it through to check for typographical and grammatical errors. Remember that most editing software will have built-in spellcheckers to alert you to these, so don't ignore them. If grammar is not your strong point, there are some useful websites that can help you avoid grammatical pitfalls. A good example is www.roget.org

Remember that you will need to include a sign-off. It may just be a link back to your website if posting on your own blog, or a fuller one containing a short bio if writing a guest blog.

WHAT ARE YOU OFFERING?

One popular option is to include a special offer or competition. It's rather like those member-get-member incentives you see from time to time; it's how organizations like gyms build their membership. You can do the same with your blog, offering your regular subscriber something in return for introducing others. Of course, competitions and offers will need to be added to your own website, with a link back to the relevant page from your blog posting.

But not every blog you post will carry so obvious an incentive. Sometimes, particularly if you work in a technical field, sharing some tips, hints or shortcuts will be enough.

What you are trying to do is to give your reader a competitive advantage.

Finally, sometimes entertainment value is enough to make a blog popular. This is clearly far easier for a professional comedian than for a concrete specialist. Try, but without trying too hard, to make your blogs entertaining.

Key idea: Consider the benefits for the reader

Every article you post has to have a clear benefit that will be obvious and relevant to your target reader. Otherwise it will simply never be read. Better still is that your blog post is of such value that your readers will feel compelled to share it; that is how you grow your audience.

Categories and tags

It's important to assign your posts to categories and tag them. This will not only help your readers find relevant posts on your blog, but will improve how search engines list your posts in results. Don't try to assign irrelevant categories or tags to posts, as this will confuse your readers and won't encourage them to subscribe or come back to read your new posts.

As we mentioned in the section on the benefits of blogging, search engines like Google use these tags when listing sites on their results pages. They're smart, though, so don't think they won't pick up on irrelevant tags that don't match the content of your post. This is why it's important to use plenty of relevant tags (or keywords) – they will improve your blog's SEO and help you get listed more, and in more prominent positions on search engine results pages (SERPs).

Just one post won't get you ranking high in search engines, though – they use frequency and amount of posts to judge you on credibility, so expect to maintain your blog properly before noticing any improved levels of traffic coming to your blog from search engines.

Try it now: Write your first blog post!

Draft your first blog post using the tips we have mentioned above and incorporating the writing standards and etiquette we covered in Chapter 1. Get someone to read through it first and then develop the article, using any feedback you get. Then post it on your blog!

Where to find inspiration

If you find yourself worrying about what your next post is going to cover, consider the following options for finding inspiration:

▶ **Current affairs** People are more likely to be searching for current news, so relevant search terms will be popular.

▶ **Google Alerts** Get set up so that you receive an email when new search results appear for a specific phrase.

▶ **Other blogs** What are other people in your sector talking about?

▶ **Carry a notebook and camera** Jot down ideas (and take appropriate pictures) when you are out and about.

▶ **Respond to requests** Readers may request a 'how to' article or further information on a topic – keep your readers up to date on what's happening to your project. In fact, the more your future blogs are clearly the consequence of reader requests, the more responsive and therefore appealing you will become to your readers.

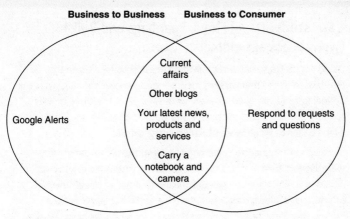

Business to Business   Business to Consumer

Current affairs

Other blogs

Your latest news, products and services

Carry a notebook and camera

Google Alerts

Respond to requests and questions

Figure 8.2 Sources of inspiration

There are also various techniques you can use to keep the content of your blog lively and fresh:

▶ **Collaborate with other bloggers and co-author posts** – these can be great if you want to show two different viewpoints or share a joint experience. These will also bring in a new audience if the other blogger or author is established elsewhere, as their audience will want to read the post on your blog.

▶ **Publish guest blogs** submitted to you from other writers – these allow a completely fresh new tone and approach to your blog's topic. As with collaborated blogs, you will draw in the guest blogger's audience.

▶ **Use a mix of media** within your posts (video, image and sound) – these will break the text up and make your blog look more welcoming and interactive.

▶ **Try running different regular features,** such as 'how to' posts or 'ten top tips' – your readers will know that these posts are coming if they are regular features and so will know when to visit your site for the latest one.

Case study: David Floyd, Beanbags and Bullsh!t (www.beanbagsandbullsh1t.com)

David set up his social enterprise blog in 2009 to face a gap that he felt existed in the mainstream media – who was questioning what the politicians and so-called 'experts' were saying? At the time, he was running his own social enterprise and wanted an outlet to question and even challenge what he was hearing in the media.

Initially he struggled to write regularly, and the blog's early posts were, he felt, simply notes to himself rather than articles other people would actually want to read. Compelled to react to press coverage of politicians' views on social enterprise and what 'experts' were saying, David started responding to them on a regular basis. He was encouraged by regular comments on his blog and positive feedback from people at events saying they had read his articles.

David's background is in journalism and community publishing, so he has the experience and skills to have made Beanbags into a deliberately journalistic blog. Each edition sees him responding to social enterprise comment from other sources. He usually starts with a quote that has caught his eye from these articles and then proceeds to respond to it.

'I aim to be provocative,' he says, 'not in terms of being rude on a personal level, even if you are in the right – insulting people makes you look stupid – but in terms of challenging ideas in a way that leaves space for disagreement and hopefully encourages people to post comments and argue with me.

'I also write posts based on reading and responding to think-tank reports or reporting on events I've been to. I have about ten decent ideas a week for posts. I only have time to actually write one a week on average.

'Beanbags has developed its own style over the three years I've been writing it. It's less off-the-cuff now than when I started. Once you know there are at least a few people reading it, there's pressure to make sure it's not rubbish.

'I also increasingly take care (and time) to avoid making lots of assertions. It's fine to state your opinion about something but if you are saying "this government scheme is a waste of money" you need to make sure you can back this up with the facts about how much they have spent and what they have spent it on – and an example of something else that they could have spent it on instead.'

David is empowered by the freedom writing a blog gives him. However, while there's no editor or subeditor involved to cut away at what he wants to say, there's also no one to stop him from publishing something that's not up to his usual high standard.

Beanbags started out as a way for David to collect his thoughts about what he was hearing. It has developed into a regular way for him to show his support for social enterprise as a whole, encouraging everyone to 'work together to find more entrepreneurial solutions to social problems and to build a more socially just economic system overall'.

Comments

All blogging platforms have the function of allowing comments on your blog. You can edit your settings so that comments can be switched off or you can moderate them before they are published on your site. This means that you will get a notification each time a comment is posted and you will need to approve it before it gets displayed on your site (it won't be done automatically).

This is useful to keep spammers at bay, as you can simply delete these comments before they reach your blog. It also means that you can read comments first before they are published.

Remember this: Encourage comments

Allowing comments on your blog really helps boost the relationship you have with your audience, as you can engage in discussions with them and gain valuable feedback. You should always encourage comments and respond quickly to them – even if it's just a quick note to thank the commenter for taking the time to read and comment on the post. Stay upbeat when responding to negative comments and keep from inflaming a dangerous situation.

On blogs

Robert says...

To blog or not to blog, that is the question. Of course, Shakespeare would have been an ardent blogger. Blogging provides almost instant interaction between writer and reader. I have a number of blogs, too many really, and find that some rise and others fall by the wayside.

One of my current blogs charts my journey through to my 58th year. I'm doing 57 different things I've never done before while aged 57. It's light-hearted, but the book that I hope will follow will have a serious message: you have to try harder to explore as you get older.

Some bloggers have no plan to write anything more. They provide a running commentary, often with some depth, on relevant – and often local – current affairs. Jason Cobb of Colchester Chronicle (www.colchesterchronicle.co.uk) is one of my favourites. Even those who find his blogs uncomfortable consider each post to be a compelling read. Jason's not part of the Establishment, nor has anyone given him the right to write. But he does it anyway and that's the appeal.

I'm not as bold, preferring instead to explore topics and themes, often by adding comments to other people's blogs, rather than always trying to attract people to my own.

I blog from trains. It works for me and a short journey means a word-count limit. I like the form, I like the discipline and I love the interaction.

Summary

You should have now successfully written and published your first blog post. It might be that you have started your own blog or you have submitted content to be a guest blogger on another site. Either way, you have taken an important step in improving your online writing ability and increasing your online communication.

Commentating

In this chapter you will learn:

▶ *about the various types of commentating available to you on the Web – from online newspapers and journals to user groups and case studies*

▶ *how to tailor your writing skills to each one, to create engaging, accessible copy that gets you noticed.*

As in previous chapters, use the diagnostic test below to assess where you are now in relation to commentating on the Web.

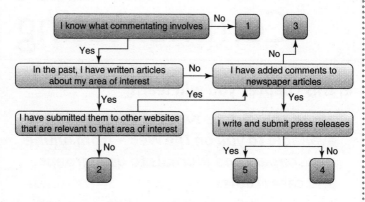

Feedback

1 Don't worry – in this chapter we will take you through the different ways you can go about commentating on a subject and how to write these comments.

2 If you have written articles that would be of interest to other people, there's no reason why you shouldn't submit them to relevant sites that would publish them.

3 These can be a great way to increase traffic to your website or link to another relevant article you have written that readers of a newspaper article would also read. We have covered this type of commentary further on in the chapter.

4 While you may not have any news to report on at the moment, there may come a time when you will, so it's best to be prepared with how to write and present press releases. It's all covered in this chapter.

5 This is good. You are commentating in various different ways – read further to make sure you are doing it correctly. There could be some areas in which you could make improvements!

The power of the word

'Nothing travels faster than the speed of light with the possible exception of bad news, which obeys its own special laws.'

Douglas Adams

If there is one thing that the Internet has given us, it is information. Whereas once we relied on newspapers, TV and radio for news, today it streams across our computer desktop the moment it is created. It is quite common for world events to be reported online by ordinary individuals, long before the media pick up the story.

The American special forces assault that led to the killing of Osama bin Laden in 2011 was reported first by a neighbour watching the drama unfold from a nearby house. The Arab Spring uprisings that began in the same year were coordinated using online social media networks, accessed by mobile phone. The authorities were unable to suppress the spread of information.

And business events, scandals, crises and success stories are also reported online by those taking part. The way to be in the news today is to write the news today.

Every publication, TV or radio station or professional organization website is hungry for information. Advertising revenue is rarely enough to cover the cost of gathering the information; journalists are expensive and increasingly focus their time providing comment and interpretation. Even the largest regional newspaper or industry specialist journal can only afford to cover the big stories with their own reporting staff.

Your opportunity is to contribute to the growing, vast body of online knowledge. Articles you write, press coverage you secure and comments you post may remain online for a very long time. People searching for those topics will find your comments and thereby discover you!

And that is how you can grow your reputation, get to be considered an authority in your field and become far more attractive to potential new employers, customers and more.

Where to write

In the other chapters, the answer to this question is obvious. But in this chapter we are going to look at you as a commentator. So we will not be looking at one particular application such as Facebook, LinkedIn or Twitter. Instead, we will focus on writing what essentially can be considered news pieces. You may post these as articles, submit them as news releases, or simply use the techniques we will cover to make sure that comments you add are relevant.

It doesn't matter whether you are writing content for your organization's website or intranet, or material that will be published for a wider audience. The techniques will be very much the same.

Remember this: Make your commentating accessible

However technical the subject, there is no excuse for writing dense and difficult-to-read material. Always assume that your reader knows very little about the subject and write accordingly. That does not mean using lots of words to describe basics of your subject. It's more about being clear, concise and explaining technical terms and acronyms. It is also good practice to reference your writing with hyperlinks to more detailed explanations of the points you are making.

Let's now take a look at some of the different places where you might be writing words for the Web.

Newspapers

Traditionally, newspapers were the place where everybody looked to find out what was happening in the world. Today newspapers are less important, not least because things are reported first online, then on radio and TV and finally in print. But what this has meant is that newspapers have become increasingly focused on comment. In other words, the newspaper may not necessarily be where you find out about the story first, but it may well be where you come to truly understand its context and implications.

This actually increases your opportunity to have your views published in print. Although you will be writing with an aim of getting your comments on the newspaper's online comment pages, you may very well find them printed, too. For example, imagine that you are the HR manager for a large firm employing 500 people in your city. There is a national story that emerges about how some unscrupulous employers are short-changing their staff when they claim maternity benefits. Your local newspaper will be keen to give its readers a local slant on this national story. Your job, location and the size of your team qualify you to provide an expert comment on the story. This is what you might write and email over to the editor:

> Like you, I was shocked to read this morning about the way some employers are short-changing their staff, particularly pregnant women claiming maternity benefit. I guess you will be covering the story yourself in tomorrow's edition and so I thought you might find the following comment useful:
>
> A good number of our 500 staff are young women and so at any one time we will have up to 10 people on maternity leave. As responsible employers, we work very hard to make sure that, at this special time in their lives, we offer our staff as much support as we possibly can. It is appalling to think that some employers would take advantage of people at this time.
>
> I suspect that most large organizations are like our own, in that our staff forms quite a tight-knit community. It would be short-sighted to mistreat those who were not at work because it would be hugely demotivating to the rest of the team. So not only is treating pregnant staff the right thing and ethical thing to do; it is also an investment in the motivation of the entire team.

What you have done by issuing this comment is made it clear that not only do you support your staff at a time of vulnerability, but you have a clear commercial reason for doing so. Setting aside the ethical aspects of the story, you are also calling into question the commercial judgement of the reported company.

Remember that to comment you need to be able to speak from a position of authority, experience and/or significance:

▶ **authority** – you are recognized as someone who knows their subject (e.g. a senior HR manager)

▶ **experience** – people will know that you have directly relevant experience of the subject (e.g. you employ 500 people)

▶ **significance** – this is the reason your comment will carry more weight than that of others (e.g. you are the largest employer in town).

Try it now: Write a short comment

Look online for the website of your local newspaper or trade publication and find a story about which you have something useful to say. It might be a story critical about one of your competitors, or just an upbeat report about growth in your sector, or even a story about one of the nationally influential people in your profession.

Remember that the local or trade publication will want to put their own local sector slant on the story. Your comments need to be short and to contain three key messages:

✻ your interpretation of the story
✻ how what you do is better, and why
✻ a couple of supporting facts to add credibility.

Now have a go yourself. Try to keep your comment to fewer than 150 words. The journalist will always come back to you if they want more information or to write a full feature. What's important when you comment is to be quick, accurate and on message.

Professional journals

These are very similar to newspapers, except that they will carry far more opinion and far less news. This is because they operate on far longer editorial deadlines. The journalists writing a professional magazine would do far more work when researching their original story. If you are known to them, they may well ask you for a comment when they are writing a piece. It is far harder to encourage them to publish a comment because, by then, they will have moved on from that topic and be focused on something completely different.

The exception to the rule with professional journals is the letters page. The cynic would say that the more letters a magazine publishes in response to its editorial content, the better able it is to reassure its advertisers that the magazine is read. An editor would say that reader feedback is crucially important because it allows the magazine to show that it has its finger on the pulse of the profession or industry it reports on.

Writing a letter to the editor is usually the best way to comment in the professional press. And, although they are called 'letters', they are of course always sent by email! Every publication will have an email address to which you can send letters. Most commonly, it is letters@thepublicationtitle.co.uk, although sometimes you will be asked to send your email to a named member of the editorial team.

Writing a letter is very similar to writing a comment. The key difference between the two is that sometimes the best letters are the shortest. When you write a comment for a newspaper you want it to be long enough to be clearly visible on the page; that way, people will spot your name and your words far more readily in the follow-up story. But a letter is different. The editor will want to feature as many letters as possible on a dedicated website and in print, and will also want to avoid having to edit letters down. Even 150 words is too long for a letter.

In fact, some of the best letters are the shortest, so think of letter writing rather as you would think of tweeting. Try to compress your comment into 140 characters. This will translate into three or four lines on the page of a typical four-column magazine.

Take a look at the earlier example of the story about the mistreatment of staff on maternity leave. This is how the comment might translate into a letter to the editor:

> Sir,
>
> I'm appalled. We employ 500 women. The better we treat staff on maternity leave, the happier our close-knit team becomes. It's common sense!
>
> Jack Daw
>
> HR Manager
>
> Brick & Sons Ltd

A top tip is to always have a highlighter pen with you when reading newspapers and magazines. You can then mark the articles about which you can make a comment. If you do this as a matter of habit, replying within a day or two of receiving the publication, you will soon find your comments being picked up and used.

Consider it a more work-focused use of your coffee break than completing the crossword.

Popular blogs

We have already talked about how to set up and write your own blog. Now we will look at how to piggyback your message on to successful blogs written by other people.

There are a number of key benefits of doing this:

▶ You benefit from access to someone else's.

▶ Your comments will inevitably be read by the blog author.

▶ You can add hyperlinks in your comment back to your own website.

But none of these benefits will be gained if your comment is too overtly promotional, either of you or your company. Many blogs – in fact, most of the better ones – will moderate comments before they are posted on the website. This means that, unless your comment is approved, it will not appear.

When I comment on the blogs written by other people I do so with three clear objectives:

1 to endorse or challenge points made in the blog and publicly associate myself with that view

2 to get noticed by the author of the blog to whom I often send an introductory email after my comment has been published

3 to encourage other readers of the blog to link to an article I have written elsewhere or, more usually, to the website of a project on which I am working.

Here are some techniques to help you post comments on to other people's blogs that will get you noticed.

IDENTITY

There is no point in posting a comment unless you can be clearly identified as its author. Sometimes people are registered with blogging websites under an alias. Perhaps you have a personal blog for which you use a pen name, which is hosted in the same place as the blog upon which you wish to comment. As a default, you will be invited to comment under your alias, not your actual name. You may need to set up a separate account to easily and quickly add comments as yourself.

I prefer, because essentially I work alone, to sign off my comments on other people's blogs as: Robert Ashton www.robertashton.co.uk. This will encourage people to click through to my website when they have read my comment. This is exactly what I want them to do.

Finally, most blogging websites will ask you to upload a photograph as well as your name. Always use a good head-and-shoulders picture because people will look at the photograph before they read your name. Be consistent and use the same image across all online platforms. This will help you build your personal brand.

CONTENT

As with all business writing, the fewer words you use the greater the impact of your comment will be. This is true even if you have a lot you want to say. People will only read around

200 words before pausing. (That is why this book is full of sections, to break up your journey into bite-sized chunks.)

If the point you want to make cannot be fully covered in 200 words, your comment should be a summary of your point, with links to more detailed content elsewhere. Some commentators write copious amounts but you may discover that this actually works for them only because they are a specialist in that field. As a rule of thumb, however, I would advise you to stick to 200 words.

Key idea: The good comment

There are three sections that make up a good comment:
1 Your main point should come first and should contain keywords from the blog itself.
2 Next, expand your point to really emphasize what you want to say.
3 Draw a conclusion and perhaps challenge other commentators to respond.

PROMOTE

This final point is both obvious and often overlooked. The whole point of adding comments to other people's blogs is to be noticed and read by a wider audience. So, having written and submitted your comment, as soon as it is published you should share it as widely as possible.

You can do this across a number of platforms, for example:

▶ by tweeting a link to your followers, being sure to copy the author of the original blog (using their Twitter identity – @whoever)

▶ by posting a comment on your Facebook page and including the link to your comment or to the blog itself (Facebook conveniently displays a summary of the page automatically when it is linked to in an update)

▶ by sharing an update to your LinkedIn profile, clicking on the 'Attach a link' button to share your comment with your LinkedIn audience.

Try it now: Comment on a blog

✻ Find some blogs about subjects that interest you. They don't have to be all work-related; some could be about favourite hobbies and pastimes. This means that each time a new blog is posted, the first couple of lines will appear on your Google home page.

✻ Next, find recent blogs that are particularly relevant to you. Best of all is to find blogs that make you angry or excited. The stronger you feel about something, the more passionate and powerful your writing will become.

✻ Finally, write your comment. As with everything else, it does not have to be long, but it must be relevant. Again, use words from within the blog in your comment. This demonstrates that you have read it before commenting. This is particularly important because many blogs are moderated. That means someone will check your comment before allowing it to appear on the bottom of the blog.

Remember this: Amazon reviews are comments, too

Posting a review on Amazon of a book or a product is basically the same as posting a comment on a blog. All the same rules apply when writing your comment. A top tip is that, when asked for your location, place your website address here instead. This should result in your Web address appearing underneath your name with your review.

Posting an Amazon review, particularly about a book, is a really good way to win favours from authors! But, seriously, when you post the Amazon review, you are invited to recommend other products you think might appeal to people buying the product you have just reviewed. This clearly gives you the opportunity to comment on something which sells very well and to link those who view that page to something of yours which might be less well known.

Hyper local websites

If your job involves you in local community affairs, or if you are one of those people who get involved in things in the neighbourhood where you live, you need to be active on hyper local websites.

They are a relatively new phenomenon. They go beyond the kind of local activity you see on Facebook or Twitter. They are websites that use mapping very cleverly to encourage neighbours to share thoughts, ideas and opportunities with each other. They are brilliant platforms upon which campaigns can be built.

If you visit the website www.openlylocal.co.uk, you will be able to find your local hyper local website. They are almost always independently run and cover a very small geographical area. For example, http://openlylocal.com/hyperlocal_sites/883-Port-Talbot-Magnet covers an area within six miles of Port Talbot, in Wales. It is run as a cooperative, providing news, information and opportunities for people to find others with similar interests or concerns.

Streetlife (www.streetlife.com) is a good example of a hyper local network. Rather than being volunteer-led, Streetlife has the backing of a major newspaper publishing group. People sign up using their postcode and soon find themselves connecting with neighbours and local businesses. Unlike location-specific hyper local websites, Streetlife members can check out and connect with people in other communities. This could be really useful if you have a business which covers a number of locations.

INTERACTING

The key point to remember with hyper local websites is that they are community-based and community-driven. Users will be intolerant of blatant sales promotion. It is no good posting that you are offering a two-for-one deal at your restaurant or that you are looking for a job.

Instead, your contribution needs to be conversational in style. For example:

> User post by Jane:
>
> We have been thinking of putting a conservatory on to the back of our house. Who has one already, is pleased with it and could recommend a supplier?

Your company makes conservatories. You spot the entry and decide to comment:

> *Bad comment:* Hi Jane, we make conservatories and would love to come and talk to you about yours. We have a special deal on conservatory blinds at the moment. When can I come round?

> *Good comment:* Hi Jane, it is always a good idea to talk to people who already have a conservatory before choosing a supplier. We have worked recently in your neighbourhood, so if you don't find people to speak to here, let me know and I will introduce you to some of our satisfied customers.

The good comment is far less pushy and far more focused on meeting Jane's needs. You are being honest and saying that you supply conservatories. But you are also saying nothing about your product, or trying to push it on to Jane. Instead, you are suggesting that you are confident enough in your product to introduce customers so that Jane can find out about your company from them.

The same rule of thumb should be applied no matter what it is that has prompted you to comment. Your comment should be written to help and encourage the debate, not converted into a sales presentation for anything you may be keen to promote.

Remember this: Be generous!

The more freely you give your time, knowledge and support, the more popular you will become. People will always want to work, mix and do business with popular people. Paradoxically, by putting others first, particularly in community forums such as hyper local websites, you will be doing yourself a huge favour.

Networking of any kind is like opening a bank account. You need to invest before you can make any kind of withdrawal or earn any interest!

User groups

Particularly if you work in a technical environment, there will be user groups, often hosted on supplier websites which you will be invited to join. For example, if you use a particular piece of software or technology, there will be user groups (formal and informal) where people share tips, information and advice.

Many of the rules we have discussed so far will apply to these closed user groups, specifically the following:

▶ **Be positive** – and look for solutions rather than criticizing shortcomings.

▶ **Be concise** – and use hyperlinks to more detailed content where necessary.

▶ **Be helpful** – and share shortcuts and tips you have discovered.

▶ **Be consistent** – even when you are busy, try not to neglect a strand of conversation that you have started.

Being an active member of a user group can do a lot for your reputation. This is particularly true if you work in a backroom environment and do not have a lot of contact with customers, suppliers or others working in your professional or business sector.

When adding content to user groups, it is OK to use technical jargon and acronyms. That's because your audience will be people who understand that technical language. However, be careful not to assume that your readers will know as much about the subject as you do. Indeed, if you are to be seen as an expert, you will need to write it in a way that translates the complicated into the relatively simple.

It can be very tempting, when discussing complicated specific issues with like-minded people, to slip out of speaking in basic terms. Never forget that you also need to make your writing accessible to the casual reader.

> **Remember this:** Avoid 'geek speak' as far as possible
>
> If you write in 'geek speak', you will be limiting your audience to those who understand the terminology you are using.

Writing case studies

A great way to illustrate your point is to write a case study. Case studies are credible because they tell stories. People like to read stories about the experiences of others. Storytelling is the way everything was taught before written language evolved.

There is a technique to writing a good case study. It is very much like writing a press release in that it needs to be relatively short, simple and follow a logical progression. It is very tempting, when writing case studies, to add in lots of detail. But detail can make a case study lengthy and difficult to read.

The purpose of a case study is to illustrate how something works. Specifically, each case study you write should highlight one single benefit that you want to communicate to your reader.

For example:

▶ a recruitment consultant might want to show how the candidates they help stay with the companies that hire them

▶ a car dealer might want to show how good they are at after-sales support

▶ a project manager in a local government department might want to show colleagues the benefits to them of regular and timely reporting.

When a subject is written as a case study, it is always more believable than if simply written as descriptive text. That said, case studies do need to be written honestly and not be works of fiction, however tempting that may appear!

The length of a case study will vary according to the place where it is to appear. For example, the case studies in this book are all around 200 words in length. Case studies for a website should be of a similar length. A magazine or journal case study could be three or four times longer.

Whatever its length, every case study should follow the following formula.

TITLE

The title or headline of your case study should capture the key point you are trying to communicate in just one sentence. A case study should tell your story through the experiences of others. A good tip is to include the word 'says' in the title. For example: 'My geranium window boxes from Highway Nurseries are blooming marvellous, says local hotelier'.

INTRODUCTION

Next, you need to tell the story in one paragraph. This is important because most people will read the first paragraph before deciding whether to go further. If your case study is published online, then the title and first paragraph may be all that people see before clicking to reveal the full piece.

When writing your introductory paragraph, you need to ask yourself: who, what, how, why, where and when? The more these points are explained in that first paragraph, the more you will hook your reader and encourage them to read further. For example:

> 'James Birch hated climbing ladders and decided to try the new self-watering window-box system he was offered by Highway Nurseries. As well as saving time, the window boxes kept their geraniums fresh all season. "We pick up a lot of passing trade," James said, "and so it is important that the front of the hotel always looks cared for and inviting."

THE STORY

Now you need to tell the full story, being sure to expand on who, what, how, why, where and when. As far as possible, the case study should be written as if being described by the subject of the story. You are the narrator, but your subject is the person who provides the direct quotes. The introductory paragraph above shows you how this works.

This section of your case study can be as short or as long as necessary, within the bounds of the space available. That said, remember the point we have made many times in this book: fewer words usually convey more impact and meaning.

On a practical note, it is unlikely that the person you are writing about will provide the right comments for you to include in the case study. You will need to draft their comments for them, then seek their approval for publication. Wherever possible, get to know your subject well enough to enable you to structure their comments using words and language they will find familiar.

CALL TO ACTION

The reason you are writing a case study is to encourage the reader to do something. The final paragraph of your case study needs to make it as appealing as possible for the reader to react in the way you would wish them to. Clearly, this cannot be a blatant invitation to make a purchase or change behaviour. It needs to be direct, but not *so* direct that it comes over as a command or pushy sales pitch.

A good way to get the point across is to use the voice of the person the case study is written about to make the final point. They are, in theory anyway, impartial and not influenced by your own commercial, professional or career ambition. For example:

> Not everybody hates ladders as much as James Birch but, as he explained, the return on investment in self-watering window boxes from Highway Nurseries was measurable: 'Trade was good throughout the summer,' he explained, 'and enough people commented on the window boxes for me to be confident they played an important part in bringing customers through the door.'

Case study: Rob Archer, The Career Psychologist (www.thecareerpsychologist.com)

Although Rob spent 11 years as a management consultant, he retrained as a psychologist because he wanted to develop his understanding of how people make change in their lives – and how they sustain it.

Rob now works as an occupational psychologist specializing in leadership development and assessment, coaching, organization development and resilience training. His experience spans professional services, financial services, professional sports teams, central and local government, oil, gas, construction and fast-moving consumer goods (FMCG). Rob also works with clients in an individual (coaching) capacity, in particular helping people to improve workplace performance, cope with stress or make better career decisions.

Rob writes for several blogs and has published articles about career change on various websites. All drive traffic to his website, where he promotes two main services: career change (helping people change career) and career management (helping people improve their career). By getting his views, experience and knowledge out in front of a wider audience, his website attracts more visits, which in turn increase his number of prospective clients.

Of course, the call to action will vary depending on the subject and the audience. If your case study is for in-house consumption, perhaps to encourage people to follow good practice, you can be far more direct. But, equally, you still need to avoid appearing to be too pushy. People have to want to do something without feeling they are being pushed.

BOILERPLATE

As with a news release, you need a couple of sentences at the bottom of your case study that make it easy for the reader to follow up on the story. On a news release the boilerplate summarizes the key points about the organization, as well as providing its contact details. When writing a case study, the boilerplate can be more specific and focused on helping the reader find out more about the story.

For example, this is how the boilerplate might appear for our story about James Birch and the self-watering window boxes:

> 'Highway Nurseries' self-watering window boxes cost from £25 each. For information and advice, call Highway on 01234 567890.

It is good practice to show the boilerplate a couple of lines below the case study copy and to place it in a separate text box. This enables people to see that it is not simply an extension of the case study.

On commentating

Robert says...

As an author, my credibility grows or slumps with each new book. But books take ages to write and sometimes almost as long to read. Comment is faster and, often, more responsive.

I try to make time to be a thoughtful commentator on many aspects of entrepreneurship. I want to influence policymakers, encourage practitioners and spread the word that we can all benefit from adopting an attitude of entrepreneurship.

And so I comment. As well as writing my own blogs, I volunteer articles for websites, magazines and newspapers. Each, of course, says something quite different, but inevitably all are variations on a theme.

And for me that's the power of being a commentator. It's enabling others to become aware of me and my work through a range of media. As their awareness grows, so, too, does the probability that they will mention me and perhaps even get in touch.

I often get invited to speak at events and take part in debates because of what I have written.

Focus points

✳ To comment, you need to be able to speak from a position of authority, experience or significance.

✳ Comments that appear too overtly promotional are more likely not to be published or read.

✳ Make sure readers are able to link your comments to you and that they can easily find a way to contact you or find out more – this can be done by including a link to your website each time you submit a comment.

✳ Professional journals will usually seek comment on stories before they are published – comments post-publication will usually be found on the letters page.

✳ Anything you quote from another person must be approved by them.

Summary

You have seen that similar rules apply in all online writing. However, when writing case studies, articles or comments on the articles of others, you have far more flexibility. You are not constrained, for example, by the 140-character count of Twitter. Nor are you constrained by the need always to win the support of an editor, who can choose to publish or ignore your writing.

But that does not mean to say you have free rein to speak your mind, be unconstructively critical, or even biased or rude. Everything that you write has to be capable of being substantiated by fact. People will check, ask for details, and, if you are making bold claims, challenge your standpoint.

There is just one final point we would like to make about taking part in online debate and commentary. Not everybody will see the world in the way that you do and some will choose to post deliberately destructive comments about your work.

You have only to look at the comments posted on newspaper articles online to see that some people have a very strange outlook. People who post a lot of negative, defamatory or otherwise unpleasant content are known as 'trolls'. They usually post anonymously and a number have been prosecuted for breaking the law. If you find yourself on the receiving end of comments from a troll, the only way to deal with it is to ignore it. Responding usually only makes matters worse.

Now that you have finished this chapter, it is time for you to take another look around the Internet and start being a commentator.

Afterword: Looking ahead

'I know there's a farmer out there somewhere who never wants a PC and that's fine with me.'

Bill Gates

The only certainty about the Internet is that we will all find ourselves under increasing pressure to become more active online. Every few months a new social media platform emerges that pundits consider to be 'the next big thing.'

As your friends and colleagues become users of each new platform, your email inbox fills with invitations to join their new communities. The people who create these social media communities set them up in ways that make those invitations to take part very compelling. Remember that the value of a social media website is in the number of members it attracts and the extent to which they engage.

So you have to decide the extent to which you want your life to be dominated by online activity. This is perhaps something you are already well aware of in your personal and social life. Smartphones mean that you are constantly in touch with your social networks. You know when your friends have gone shopping, where they are eating and what they are doing. The temptation to comment, share and engage in the online world is high.

At work, email is now widely recognized as being both a benefit and a curse. It is simply too easy to copy in everybody you think might be interested in your email. People also find themselves emailing colleagues across the room, rather than strolling across to their desk.

The biggest challenge we all face, as we write online, is to manage the extent to which it takes over our lives. We have to be selective in the media we choose to use. We have to be selective about what we read, because each one of us could spend an entire week reading useful and interesting content about topics important to our career.

Increasingly, the written word will be replaced by video. Articles, case studies and commentary can be far more credible when spoken rather than written. People increasingly prefer to see and hear rather than read. Increasing broadband speeds, particularly on mobile networks, will make video far more important than it is today.

Fortunately, all of the points and rules described in this book are equally appropriate to both the written and spoken word. When making a video, you need to plan what you want to say and then say it in a clear and logical way. An off-the-cuff ramble may be easy to produce, but will do you few favours when it is viewed by others.

Perhaps the greatest benefit of your online writing will be your ability to broaden your network of contacts across the globe. While writing this piece of text, I had Facebook open on my other screen. A contact of mine in Ghana messaged me for a quick chat. He has found a local bank that might sponsor me to visit his country and work with young entrepreneurs.

Our exchange of messages consisted, in total, of 80 words and was completed in four minutes. The ability to communicate quickly, effectively and consistently with people many thousands of miles away, with whom you would never be speaking without the Internet, is the single biggest benefit of being online.

Finally, with the ability to communicate instantly and effectively with people all around the world, it's all the more important that your writing is clear, concise and consistent. Increasingly, the people with whom you are communicating will use English as a second or third language. They will not be familiar with the social context within which you live and work and there will be massive opportunities for misunderstanding. However, having read this book, completed the exercises and practised the techniques, you are now far better equipped to succeed in your online world.

Good luck!

Index